# Think Like a Dog

# Think Like a Dog

## How dogs teach us to be happy in life and successful at work

Scott MacDonald, Chairman/CEO,
and Sadie, Rescue Dog

Prestyge
Books

AN IMPRINT OF
INDIANA UNIVERSITY PRESS

This book is a publication of
Prestyge Books, an imprint of

Indiana University Press
Office of Scholarly Publishing
Herman B Wells Library 350
1320 East 10th Street
Bloomington, Indiana 47405 USA

iupress.indiana.edu

Manufactured in the United States of America

Cataloging information is available from the Library of Congress.

ISBN 978-0-253-04003-9 (paperback)
ISBN 978-0-253-04005-3 (ebook)

1 2 3 4 5    24 23 22 21 20 19

*In memory of my brother and sister*
*Bing MacDonald and Judy Anderson*

*In memory of Mandy and Nanuk,*
*the four-legged members of my family, who enriched my life*
*and the lives of my siblings and children*

*In further memory of Sadie's former pack mates and pals*
*Jake and Bella and Jake's co-owner and*
*my good friend, Tom McCarthy*

"I'm telling you I'm *not* paranoid! Sometimes he only *pretends* to throw the ball just to make me look like an idiot!"

Dogs and philosophers do the greatest good and get the fewest rewards.

—DIOGENES

The more I see of representatives of the people,
the more I admire my dogs.

—ALPHONSE DE LAMARTINE

You think those dogs will not be in heaven! I tell you
they will be there long before any of us.

—ROBERT LOUIS STEVENSON

The more I see of men, the better I like dogs.

—MADAME DE STAEL

Any man who does not like dogs and want them about
does not deserve to be in the White House.

—CALVIN COOLIDGE

# CONTENTS

# Preface

**Many years ago, dogs hunted** for their food, found water in nearby rivers and streams, and were self-sufficient like their wild cousins, the wolves. As time progressed, however, dogs evolved and trained humans to hunt for them; deliver food in bowls or trays at least twice daily; provide an ample supply of clean, filtered water; take them wherever they need to go; bathe them when dirty; and obtain medical attention for them whenever needed.

At night, my dog Sadie makes herself comfortable at the foot of the master bed, lying on the memory foam mattress that conforms to her body. The bed covers are changed and cleaned regularly, and I often vacuum the piles of dog hair from the bed. In the morning, if I show signs of sleeping late, Sadie wakes me up so I can take her on her morning walk to the beach.

I take her on afternoon and evening walks, play with her, and respond to her basic needs and desires. Sometimes we deliberately stop by to visit neighbors who have treats or have dogs that like to play with Sadie.

Throughout history, domesticated dogs have served man in many roles, including hunting, herding, protection, and companionship. There has been an interesting turnabout in deciphering who really serves whom; it is becoming increasingly unclear if dog serves man or vice versa.

A couple years ago, my partner, Patti, and I visited the Roman Emperor Diocletian's Palace in Split, Croatia. The local museum there has preserved a dining area used by the emperor and Roman elite. Around AD 400, servants brought bowls of food and drink and left them on the marble dining platform. The diners lay about and ate at their leisure. Today, I bring Sadie her bowls of water and food and leave them on her floor mat, where she eats at her leisure.

In a similar vein, when I first visited the Forbidden City in Beijing, the guide explained life five hundred years ago. There was no indoor plumbing, for example. When the emperor needed to go to the bathroom, a servant appeared with a chamber pot and then removed it when the emperor was finished. I recall thinking this was not a great job. At least the servant worked directly for the emperor, however. Now, I carry plastic bags to clean up after Sadie—basically the same job the servant had in the emperor's court long ago.

How did dogs replace emperors and dog owners become the servants? Perhaps the answer lies in understanding behavioral patterns in dogs. After spending the last few years with Sadie and watching this initially timid rescue dog gradually take over my home and my life, I can share observations that may help explain the successful lifestyle of dogs. These insights illustrate how to apply the successful thinking of dogs to the challenges of the human environment.

# Introduction

## About Sadie

Beaumont, a town of about 120,000, lies between Houston and Lake Charles, Louisiana, in eastern Texas. The climate is considered subtropical, which usually means oppressive humidity, lots of rain, and very hot days. Beaumont is not a scenic city; it is a working city. It is not a wealthy city, despite its proximity to oil refineries and an active port. Environmentally, it is considered one of the most polluted areas in the United States.

Shortly after the Christmas holidays had passed and on a dreary, cool day in early January 2013, a call came in to Beaumont Animal Control. Two dogs were lying near the highway and appeared to be sick and homeless.

The police dispatched their white animal control van with big identifying letters on the side and outfitted with cages and dog constraints inside. Within minutes, the animal control officers found a female yellow Labrador retriever and her pup, estimated to be about six months old. The dogs lacked any collars or tags and were assumed to be homeless. They did not resist being lifted into the wagon, probably due to poor health and malnutrition.

Both dogs were taken to the city animal shelter and placed in kennels. Both dogs were photographed, and their pictures were posted on the city's website. When no one called to claim them, the dogs were formally put up for adoption three days later. Being in a strange kennel with many other dogs must have been particularly scary for the puppy.

Shortly thereafter, a local resident, "Jane," who runs a dog rescue service, visited the kennel and adopted Blondie, as the puppy was called. She picked up the puppy and drove her to Dowlen Road Vet Center in a nearby suburban shopping center. There,

Kelly Kays, a veterinarian, diagnosed Blondie with a variety of ailments and, over the next few days, extracted an infected tooth, removed an infected claw, performed an ovarian hysterectomy, and discovered a heartworm infection that is fatal to dogs unless aggressively treated. The underweight dog was fed and hydrated. With so many problems, Blondie may have been euthanized without the intervention of Jane and her rescue organization.

Jane later called her daughter, "Claire," who was a law student at the University of Texas (UT) in Austin and mentioned the undersized yellow Lab puppy that needed a home and some serious TLC. First Claire's friend took in Blondie, and then Claire took Blondie, but both women had other commitments and could not keep the puppy. Claire mentioned the dog to her then boyfriend, Ross, also a law student at UT, and Ross agreed to adopt the puppy even knowing she had medical issues and was especially nervous and skittish around people. Her early life evidently had not included much human contact, and her mother probably taught her to shy away from people generally.

Over the next year and a half, Sadie, as Ross named her, lived with Ross, his roommate, Matt, and Matt's dog, Duke, in a small rental house not far from the UT campus in Austin. The house had a small, unfenced yard where Duke and Sadie could play when Ross or Matt were home. The boys took the dogs for walks in the neighborhood of single-family homes and grass lawns whenever they could between classes and work. Sadie adjusted to living in a house and soon grew fond of napping on Ross's bed when he was out. Her favorite activity was chasing squirrels that dared venture down from trees when she was out for a walk.

After graduating from UT law school and working for a year as a clerk for a federal judge in Austin, Ross received a job offer from a prestigious law firm in Houston. He could not move his beloved Sadie to Houston, where he knew his work hours would be long and he would not have a roommate to share dog duties.

Ross called me, his dad, in southern California and asked me to take Sadie. I was traveling extensively at the time with business interests in Australia and elsewhere and did not think I could care for a dog, but I knew Ross loved this dog, so I agreed.

In August 2014, Ross flew to San Diego with Sadie in a crate that was placed in the baggage compartment. She was terrified when we retrieved the crate and took her to my (and her new) home. She was generally afraid of changed circumstances and new people, but she also appeared to be very intelligent and observant.

The first morning, I walked Sadie to the beach with my friends Kathy Reed, Tom McCarthy, and Klaus Gubernator and their dogs, Jake and Bella. I thought Jake and Bella would provide comfort and direction for Sadie in a strange place. When we reached the beach, about a mile away and across streets, a bridge, and a couple dirt footpaths, Sadie seemed fine, so I let her off the leash to play with the other dogs. Sadie immediately turned quickly and ran away. In addition to being smart and observant, Sadie is also very fast. She ran all the way back to my house, even though she had only been there a day and had only walked the route to the beach once. When I returned home, totally panicked and convinced I had lost Ross's dog, Sadie was waiting by the side door.

Over time, Sadie has adjusted to her new home and new environs. She has become less timid as she has become accustomed to the neighbors, their dogs, and her new neighborhood. Instead of shying away from strangers, she now begs for treats when she meets someone new. She used to be terrified of Starbucks and all the people there; now she is eager to go and waits patiently for me when I go inside to buy coffee. One day we went to Starbucks when Ross was visiting, and Ross was amazed how many people leaving Starbucks greeted her by name, even if they did not know my name.

She has made lots of dog and human friends, goes to the beach every morning to play, and has completely recovered from prior medical ailments, including heartworm. She has taken over the house, with favorite couches for afternoon naps and vantage points to watch the street, and she lets me know when anyone, especially a dog, is walking by.

As our relationship developed, I began to observe her behavior and the traits that led to her successful transition from life in the wild, to life in Austin, to life in southern California. I recognized her behavior and attitude could serve as a guide to humans dealing with challenge and transition. This recognition became the genesis of this book.

## About the Author, Scott MacDonald

As CEO, acting CEO, or president of several different and typically troubled companies, I have implemented successful corporate turnaround strategies and have worked on hundreds of troubled real estate projects throughout North America, Europe, Asia, and Australia, defining solutions—often when others have failed. I am a corporate "fix it" guy to call when companies are underperforming or at risk of failure.

© Coast Highway Photography. Used with permission.

I am frequently asked for successful corporate management formulas, common techniques for fixing companies and projects, or for key strategies for sustainable corporate success. In reality, each company is different and has specific challenges and conditions. There are general concepts, however, that are useful in designing and implementing potentially successful management initiatives.

Good management concepts are applicable for any organization, not just corporations. My involvement with nonprofit organizations and my partner Patti's work in education reaffirm the universal benefits of being a good manager and using best practice tools and methods. When Patti served as principal at a primary school located on the US Marine Corps base of Camp Pendleton, her need to be organized and manage multiple situations involving students, teachers, and parents who were raising children while fighting wars in Iraq and Afghanistan required technical knowledge, diplomacy, and management skills.

Foremost among being a good manager, I have learned, is to "think like a dog." Thinking like a dog is also a good strategy for living life in general, based on my experience as a father, husband, and longtime partner.

My family had a dog even before I was born. Mandy helped raise me and was my trusty companion through my childhood. When I had children, we rescued another mixed-breed dog named Nanuk, who was my sons' close companion. Now I have Sadie and am thrilled to share her story.

This book is written as a conversation between Sadie and me, reflecting both perspectives and in both voices. I draw on my lifetime of business and personal experiences to translate Sadie's concepts and demonstrate their applicability to human lives and organizational management. Sadie's voice is in *italics,* and my voice is in standard script. A group of asterisks (* * *) separates Sadie's voice from mine.

Profits from the sale of this book provide scholarships for college students who qualify for financial aid and are willing to help others through participation in community service projects. For more information on this program, please visit macdonaldscholars.com.

"Two seconds. How long do you pretend you've swallowed a pill before spitting it out?"

# Think Like a Dog

# 1

# Looking for Treats

**Woof. My name is Sadie.** *I really love treats like dog biscuits and bones. Maybe it's because my dog food is not that appealing. I get fed hard, compressed nuggets that are not nearly as tasty as human food. Dry dog food is supposed to be good for dogs, but humans don't eat this stuff. If people can eat good-tasting, good-smelling food, why do I have to eat kibble?*

*Treats are the only relief from my boring meals. I am always on the lookout for treats, and I find them in many places. Some humans, like Shirley, who lives nearby, actually carry dog treats with them. Often, I wait for her to come out her back door in the morning. She always has treats for me. Once when she did not emerge, I managed to go inside Shirley's house to look for her. I thought maybe she forgot what time it was.*

*Joni and Van, who live down the street, also have treats—even though, like Shirley, they don't have a dog. I walk very slowly and sniff a lot whenever we are walking by their house. I am always hopeful they will come out and give me some special peanut butter treats before I pass by. I like Joni and Van a lot and let them know I appreciate them whenever I see them in the neighborhood.*

*There is a woman named Pat on the beach every morning who always has treats. While the other dogs run around and chase each other, I search for her. She usually wears a pink jacket, but yesterday she wore a white one. The change did not fool me.*

*Pat walks slowly and always follows her husband, Robert, and his dog. When I see Robert, I know Pat is coming, even when she is not yet visible. Sometimes I run off the beach and intercept Pat in the parking area. When good treats are at stake, you should never wait, because another dog may get there first.*

*Pat is older and very wary of dogs that run and jump. I realize this, so I stop and sit in front of her so she does not feel threatened. She always gives me treats but almost never gives the more active dogs anything.*

*Sometimes Pat holds out her open hands and pretends to have no treats. She can convince others, but I know better and persist. I always prevail, and she eventually gives me treats. I do not take no for an answer, especially if I can smell treats despite her protesting otherwise.*

*I have learned that Jim, Betsy, and Janet all carry treats when they walk their dogs. Usually they don't mind sharing if I ask politely and wag my tail in appreciation. The key is knowing who has treats and how best to convince them to share.*

*Sometimes there are treats lying in the street or in the bushes. I know where people drop food and am always on the alert whenever I pass through a familiar area. Interestingly, when a treat is found in a particular spot, other treats are often subsequently found in the same place. Remembering where the treats have been is always helpful.*

*People—especially children—are often careless when they eat. Sometimes I just hang around under the dinner table and am rewarded with a bouncing morsel or a wet splat of food. Even though I don't know what kinds of tidbits will appear, hanging around places where they typically fall is usually a good strategy.*

* * *

Some believe finding a treat is a matter of luck. Darrell Royal, the long-time University of Texas football coach, once said, paraphrasing a Roman philosopher, "Luck occurs when preparation meets opportunity."[1] Unless a person is looking for treats and thinking about treats, he or she probably will not find them.

In personal relationships, special treats matter. Bringing home flowers, having an impromptu celebratory dinner, or providing an unexpected gift or compliment are all personal treats that help make a relationship special.

Going on vacation with a spouse or partner is a treat that takes a couple away from the pressures of work or family. Even if the budget is limited, taking a vacation can be a special treat that will be long remembered and appreciated. It can help rebuild or strengthen a relationship, especially if the destination and setting are equally desired by both people.

There is considerable research indicating that experiences, including vacations, are more valuable "treats" for most people than tangible gifts are.[2] In a society where material possessions are widely held (the average house has about three hundred thousand items), the appreciation for receiving a material gift seems to diminish with time as other gifts are received.[3] However, memories forged during trips taken together can last for a lifetime.

Dr. Thomas Gilovich, a psychology professor at Cornell University, has studied the relationship between money and happiness. He says, "We buy things to make us happy, and we succeed. But only for a while. New things are exciting at first, but then we adapt to them."[4] He suggests that spending

Bernie is a nine-year-old dachshund terrier mix that lives near Sadie and is always on the lookout for treats. His owner, Stacy, often takes Bernie shopping with her, and Bernie knows which stores keep dog treats. One day at Z Gallerie, Bernie went to the back counter immediately after entering the store and waited for his usual treat. An older female shopper, who clearly did not like dogs, saw Bernie off his leash and yelled, "Shoo, shoo, dog!" Bernie disappeared behind the counter to get away from the woman. After the clerk gave Bernie his treat, he took the dog biscuit to the complaining woman and dropped it on her shoe. Dogs love treats, but they also love people. Bernie was trying to be nice and perhaps calm the upset woman. He also may have thought "shoo" meant "shoe"!

money on experiences, including trips, will provide greater and longer-lasting happiness. Giving someone the treat of an experience or vacation should provide lasting benefits.

Treats are important for both dogs and people. Unlike dogs, people can give themselves treats that provide personal pleasure. While on vacation in Myanmar last year, Patti bought herself a bracelet. Wearing it still gives her good feelings and memories about the trip and her ability to buy herself something so nice. Giving oneself a gift is not unusual; Stephen Lussier of De Beers recently stated in an interview that 31 percent of all diamond jewelry purchased in the United States was bought by individuals as gifts for themselves.[5]

Even small treats can provide a personal boost, a momentary sense of happiness, and a diversion from problems and challenges. Sometimes receiving such a treat can change one's outlook and ability to deal with problematic issues, especially when the treat is unexpected. Once I gave a cabinetmaker who was doing some work for me a couple of tickets to a Padres baseball game. He could have bought tickets himself—it is not difficult or expensive to buy San Diego Padres tickets—but he had not done so, as he was busy with work, and his wife had a health issue. He and his wife went and had a wonderful time; they still talk about going to the baseball game that night.

Treats also serve as a diversion from stressful activities and worries. Patti and I find that a weekend trip to Sonoma or Paso Robles to drink some wine and eat good food causes all other problems to disappear, at least for a while. For some, taking in a movie at the local cinema or even a trip to the shopping mall can have a cathartic effect on their momentary outlook. My niece Jackie, who is a nurse, calls it "retail therapy."

When dieters struggle with calorie counting and food restrictions, an occasional small chocolate treat does not have that many calories and may help them return to the path of better weight management. All dieting all the time is difficult to sustain.

It is important to recognize that different people—and dogs—like and respond to different treats. On the beach, people get excited when they find money or jewelry. Some people actually walk back and forth on the beach looking for jewelry with metal detectors. One time, Sadie followed a guy with a metal detector while he crisscrossed the beach. Pat Steusloff, a neighbor, figured Sadie thought the metal detector was really a bagel detector. For dogs, objects like jewelry are worthless. Sadie prefers a bagel or hot dog to a fancy bracelet any day. Unless one knows his or her partner, colleague, friend, or opponent very well or takes the time to learn, he or she may not know what treats to offer to elicit the desired outcome. At least with dogs, you are pretty safe offering a dog biscuit—or almost anything else that is edible.

In any organization, it is common to copy the successful methods of others. But just doing what everyone else is doing is like Sadie being content to eat dog food pellets every day without variety. The way to distinguish oneself and pull ahead of the competition is to find treats, wherever they can be found, and not be content with conventional fare.

---

### "Luck occurs when preparation meets opportunity."

---

Like dog treats, human treats are found in many different places. In business, for example, adding a new product line, buying property, adding new staff capability, expanding geographically, moving to better offices, and so forth are all potential growth-enhancing actions that add spice to the routine.

Receiving treats is always rewarding, but giving treats also brings rewards. This applies to both dogs and people.

Giving employees "treats" contributes to employee loyalty, job satisfaction, and productivity. A few strategies that I have used in companies I have managed include pizza day (free pizza for lunch—in Australia you need to include beer too), company picnics and parties, a community service day, better medical insurance, and a special bonus. At the Investa Property Group in Sydney, we successfully completed the refinancing of a $3 billion loan at a time when banks were reluctant to make property loans. Many employees were responsible for the company's excellent performance and reputation, which led to securing that loan, and in appreciation and recognition, the company paid every Investa employee (except senior executives, who didn't need the money) a special onetime bonus of $5,000. That unprecedented and unexpected payment, or treat, increased employee loyalty and helped the company become even more successful.

When I started my first professional job after graduate school, I relied on a corporate typing pool for correspondence and reports. On Saturdays, I showed up early, made coffee for the arriving typists, and dropped off donuts, which are human treats. In appreciation, the typists made sure my work was always done perfectly, even when more senior executives' work was not.

Providing a treat to a client or vendor often generates considerable goodwill. When someone asks a lawyer for help thinking through an issue or undertaking a small task, often that attorney does not charge him or her. Likewise, when a former colleague or business acquaintance asks for advice on an investment, it is frequently offered for free.

For example, I have known Barry Blumenthal, who was with Merrill Lynch in Houston, for twenty years. He has always given me good advice—for example, he advised against buying a risky stock that looked good to me, even though he would have personally benefited from receiving a commission if I had bought it. After my divorce, when my investment assets were likely below required account minimums, Barry continued to give me great service. After my financial status improved, I continued to give Barry money to invest until he retired, even after I moved to California. The relationships that result from helping each other lead to long-term business associations and, sometimes, personal friendships.

Finding treats and obtaining rewards usually does not happen by accident. Like Sadie, one should have a plan, know where treats have been found previously, understand locational trends, and use strategies to execute the proper search. Unlike dogs, most people seem surprised when they find or receive a treat. This is probably because they have not been planning, strategizing, or using their knowledge to secure the desired outcome.

Treats are not a substitute for getting the basics right. No dog lives on treats alone, and no organization survives on onetime initiatives. No relationship endures solely on surprise gifts.

Treats do make life in general much more exciting. They add the spice to life. Treats are often the highlight of a dog's day and could be what makes a human's day extra special. One should always be on the lookout for treats, or one might find oneself resigned to a life of repetition and kibble.

### Chapter Takeaways

1. Always be on the lookout for special treats.
2. Select treats that match the desires of the person receiving them.
3. Giving treats is as good as or better than getting treats.

Scott and a happy Sadie on the beach.

# 2

# Being Persistent

© Martin Bucella. Used with permission.

**When I moved to California,** *Scott insisted I stay off the beds and couches. But I know couches and beds are far more comfortable than lying on hard floors, and I can be very persistent.*

*When there are obstacles to getting what I want, it pays to be persistent. First, I slept on couches and beds when Scott was out or not looking. Whenever he caught me, I just scrambled off and disappeared for a few minutes until he calmed down. Eventually he gave up, and we worked out a deal: I was allowed on one couch but not on other couches or beds (at least not when Scott was looking). This worked for me at first; after all, "my" couch was so much softer than the floor.*

*I used to be banned from sleeping on the master bed at night. In the middle of the night, when Scott was asleep, and Patti was asleep or not home, I would* hop on the bed and curl up. When Scott woke up, he would scold me and make me jump off, but then he would always fall back asleep, and I would retake my rightful place on the bed. Eventually, Scott gave up, and now we share the big, soft bed.

Eventually, I gained access to all the beds, chairs, and sofas in the house except the big living room couch. Scott is holding out for one place where he is safe from my dog hair, but I am persistent, and he has no chance of success. Whenever he is out, I typically nap on the big couch. When I hear him returning, I scramble down and pretend I know nothing about the pile of dog hair on the sofa. When Patti is sitting on the couch, if I stare at her and whine softly, she lets me jump up and cuddle next to her. It is only a matter of time before I will win unrestricted access to everything.

Persistence is key to securing highly desired human food too. When adults sit down and prepare to consume plates piled high with good-smelling human food, I have trouble containing my excitement at participating in the family mealtime, especially when guests are here. But initially I am not welcome.

Slowly, I make my way to the dinner table, generally staying under the table and out of sight. When tidbits are dropped, I immediately clean the floor, demonstrating my value. If nothing is dropped, I often brush against a leg or even nuzzle a family member or dinner guest, trying to avoid being too obvious. Sometimes I just stare at the guest with my big, brown eyes. Eventually, I am accepted, and then I just wait for the morsels to fall or for someone to hand me a tasty tidbit under the table.

When a child, like Scott's granddaughter Claire, drops or throws food on the floor from a booster or high chair, I clean it up. I never openly celebrate whenever I secure a morsel, and I do not linger when the meal is over. And I definitely do not jump up and take Claire's food from her tray. If I did that, I would be exiled and lose access to all the good stuff that drops to me naturally. Persistence requires patience.

Unless people and dogs are persistent, they will never overcome restrictions and obstacles. They will spend their lives destined to lie on the hard floors.

\* \* \*

Persistence is an important characteristic for successful people too. Early in my career, I met a fellow from Oklahoma. I was unsure exactly what the guy did for a living, so I asked. The man replied, "I am a wall pusher."

"What's a wall pusher?" I inquired.

"Whenever you want to accomplish something, there is always someone in the way. It is like confronting a series of walls or obstacles that need to be pushed aside to progress. However, there is always someone on the other side of every wall pushing back, impeding progress. So, I keep pushing until the guy on the other side gets bored and goes away. That's what I do—I make things happen."

Persistence can also be important in finding the right relationship. When I first met my partner, Patti, long after our respective divorces, she was not interested in pursuing a relationship. She was focused more on reconnecting with an old boyfriend. But we stayed in touch, and eventually she realized I was a better option, so we began dating. Now we are a couple. Fortunately, I was persistent and didn't give up when initially rejected.

In life, persistence in seeking what one believes is right and best and working to overcome obstacles can lead to great success. In relationships, it takes two to build a desired union, however, and if one is uninterested despite the best efforts of the other, persistence may not lead to the desired outcome. Persistence in the face of certain defeat or rejection is not acceptable or rewarding behavior.

Many have talked about the importance of persistence in life. President Calvin Coolidge is credited with writing, "Nothing in the world can take the place of persistence. Talent will not; nothing is more common than unsuccessful men with talent. Genius will not; unrewarded genius is almost a proverb. Education will not; the world is full of educated derelicts. Persistence and determination alone are omnipotent."[1] The quote also appeared on the cover of Coolidge's memorial service program.

There are so many examples of persistence in everyday life. My nephew Wade had a challenging youth, including suffering from substance abuse. But he managed to turn his life around, went to college, and is now a highly regarded teacher in Los Angeles. His wife, Jackie, had her heart set on attending the University of California at Berkeley but was initially rejected. Persistence paid off; she was subsequently admitted and graduated from Berkeley four years later.

Persistence is required when looking for a job—especially a first job, when the applicant has little or no experience. Identifying the opportunity, finding the person who makes the hiring decision, and then connecting with her or him can often require extreme persistence. Sometimes making friends with that person's assistant can be helpful.

Persistence is helpful when one wants to buy a house but the housing market is rapidly rising; it is difficult to find the right house in a seller's market. However, acting too quickly and feeling pressure to buy now because prices are rising often leads to overpaying or securing a house that is not as suitable as desired. The phrase "Patience is a virtue" dates back to the fourteenth century but is still true today.

There are also many well-known examples of perseverance in the face of doubt and skepticism. One of my favorites is the story of George Mitchell. He was born to Greek immigrant parents in Galveston, Texas. Initially, the family lived above the shoeshine store that his father owned. George went to college at Texas A&M University and later started Mitchell Energy and Development Company, which eventually participated in the drilling of over one thousand wildcat oil and gas wells.

In the 1980s and continuing into the 1990s, Mitchell was determined to find a way to extract oil and gas from the widely available shale formations in Texas. Others in the industry doubted the likelihood of success and were critical of his dogged perseverance. In 1997, when I was living in Houston, Mitchell sold his big real estate development, the Woodlands, located just north of Houston, to an investment fund managed by my colleagues at Morgan Stanley. He sold, in part, to conserve funds for his shale research and development effort. Mitchell's focus on shale development was an all-consuming effort despite the lack of industry support or encouragement.

Eventually, Mitchell developed a technique using hydraulic fracturing and horizontal drilling that is widely utilized today to frack shale formations. Regardless of one's environmental views on fracking, Mitchell's perseverance has changed the world by making vast new supplies of oil and gas available and effectively making the United States energy independent.

There are many examples of perseverance in medicine, and one of the most prominent examples is that of Jonas Salk. Polio was a crippling disease dating back to early Egyptian times, but it was particularly feared in the 1900s. In 1952, the polio epidemic in the United States resulted in more than three thousand deaths and over twenty-one thousand victims left with partial or full paralysis.

Jonas Salk was born of Jewish Polish immigrant parents in East Harlem, New York. His father was a garment worker. After graduating from college and medical school, Salk served on the faculty of the University of Michigan and then the University of Pittsburgh, where he assumed responsibility for a laboratory that was in poor condition and had limited research capacity. He redeveloped the laboratory into a first-class facility that provided critical support for his research efforts.

Salk began an intensive focus on developing a polio vaccine. Most of his colleagues were skeptical; he was not well known at the time, his focus on using killed viruses seemed dubious, and better-known researchers were using other methods thought to be more promising. Despite the doubt and professional skepticism, Salk did develop a polio vaccine successfully; it was introduced in 1955. By 1961, the number of polio incidents had been reduced by 96 percent.

---

## Sometimes, one cannot accept no for an answer.

---

In business, as in medicine and other fields, when nontraditional solutions to difficult problems are proposed, the typical responses are "You can't do that" or "That's not the way we do it."

No one should accept either response. Just because a proposed action is not typical does not mean it is not the best and most appropriate action. Many of my work assignments through the years have been corporate workouts or turnarounds where traditional solutions have failed. That has forced my colleagues and me to look for innovative answers, but it is always surprising how resistant many are to straying from the established path. There is an old saying that has been attributed to Henry Ford and others: "If you always do what you have always done, you'll always get what you have always gotten."[2] At least until things change, and then you may receive nothing at all.

Ignoring traditional solutions often leads to better outcomes, but it takes persistence to overcome resistance from those more comfortable with traditional ways and methods. When Plaza Properties of America (PPA) was created as the spin-off of Trizec Hahn Centers in the late 1990s, the new company owned a portfolio of money-losing secondary regional shopping malls. We instituted a series of organizational changes. Greater responsibility was given to the on-site managers in the field at the expense of layers of management and controls at company headquarters. In-house leasing agents were paid commissions for deals instead of receiving a straight salary. Industry executives cautioned, "Field guys don't have the training or talent; it

 Ruby is a basset hound who often walks on the beach in the morning with his owner, Nancy. Ruby has a deep-throated bark and often irritates everyone when he is excited and barks too much. Most of us thought Ruby was kind of dumb, but one day Ruby amazed everyone. A wealthy man who lives in a big house right on the beach likes to eat breakfast on his patio overlooking the ocean. Ruby evidently carefully observed this behavior, and Ruby was persistent. One morning, the man left his bowl of cereal on the low table while he returned inside to get his coffee. By the time he reemerged, coffee in hand, Ruby had climbed up on the patio and polished off the entire bowl of cereal. Ruby had patiently waited for the right moment and was so proud of himself that he howled in delight, further aggravating the rich guy.

won't work." They also said, "Leasing guys will do bad deals just to secure commissions; it will be a disaster." They advocated tight central control, as had been the policy. What happened? Plaza Properties ignored the "expert" advice, listened to our employees, persisted in what we thought was a better way, and implemented the changes. PPA went from losing $5 million per annum to profitability in less than a year.

Sometimes, one cannot accept no for an answer. At Investa, we needed to refinance a $650 million office portfolio during the financial crisis in 2009, and the banks did not want to participate. I met with the senior lenders at one key bank, and the senior executive there said, after a long conversation, "My first answer is no. My second answer is no. My third answer is no. Now, what don't you understand?"

To which I replied, "Your first three answers do not work, so we need to start working on the fourth." Eventually, the bank did participate in the refinancing, and its participation was critical to keep the other participating banks onboard, which saved Investa from going into default.

There are many stories in sports about players who did not succeed at first but, with persistence and considerable effort, did ultimately succeed. They did not accept no for an answer. Probably the best example is the story of Michael Jordan, who did not make his high school basketball team as a sophomore. Jordan, probably the greatest basketball player in history, won six NBA titles, five NBA MVP awards, scored thirty-two thousand points, and made the winning basket in the NCAA title game for my alma mater's University of North Carolina Tar Heels. After failing to make his high school basketball team, he did not give up; instead, he redoubled his efforts to become a better basketball player and succeeded beyond any reasonable expectation.

More recently, the star basketball player Steph Curry graduated from high school in Charlotte, North Carolina, but was not recruited or offered a basketball scholarship by any major university. He chose to attend nearby Davidson College, a school with just 1,600 students, at the same time my son Ross was a student there. While at Davidson, Steph worked hard and developed a highly accurate three-point shot. Steph has since become a star player in the NBA and achieved league MVP with the champion Golden State Warriors.

Persistence is a common trait found in refugees. They typically must overcome great challenges while escaping dangerous living conditions and entering new societies for which they are unprepared. The new environs are often extremely different culturally, require a different language, and typically offer accommodation at the bottom of the economic spectrum. For example, beginning in 1975 with the fall of Saigon to North Vietnam, about 125,000 Vietnamese refugees immigrated to the United States. Later another approximately 750,000 refugees fled Vietnam for the United States. Despite having virtually no material goods (especially the boat people who came after the first wave of immigrants), speaking a foreign language, and being unemployed or employed only at an unskilled level, the refugees and their children have succeeded in adapting to their new, strange environs. Lanh Tran, vice president of First Republic Bank and treasurer of my local Rotary Club, is the daughter of Vietnamese refugees. On average, Vietnamese children in the United States outperform children born of US parents, despite the many obstacles they had to overcome.

If one's persistence leads to success, one should accept the victory without dwelling on it or lingering. When I was a young man starting my career, I met a fellow on an airplane who sold vacuum cleaners door to door. When I inquired what made the salesman successful, I was told, "After you make the sale, get out of the house!" Otherwise, the buyer may reconsider.

> ## "It's not the size of the dog in the fight; it's the size of the fight in the dog."

Colin Powell is one of the men I most admire. I have heard him speak many times, including when he swore in my son Andrew as a foreign service officer when Powell was secretary of state. Colin Powell was born to Jamaican immigrant parents in Harlem, New York. He was raised in South Bronx and worked in a furniture store while attending high school. Subsequently, he rose to become a four-star general in the US Army, chairman of the Joint Chiefs of Staff, and US secretary of state. Speaking of success, he said, "It is the result of preparation, hard work, learning from failure."[3]

A well-known quote that is commonly credited to Mark Twain but appeared in a 1911 publication and has been repeated by various people, including President Dwight D. Eisenhower, is applicable to dogs and people: "It's not the size of the dog in the fight; it's the size of the fight in the dog."[4] Persistence and determination when confronted with obstacles and setbacks are essential characteristics for success whether one is a dog or a person.

### Chapter Takeaways

1. To overcome obstacles and achieve what is desired, persistence is essential.
2. Success is rarely instant; it requires preparation and perseverance.
3. Success sometimes requires refusing to take no for an answer.

## Dogs as Poker Players

There is a famous series of paintings by the American artist Cassius Marcellus Coolidge, sometimes known as Kash Koolidge, beginning in 1894. The paintings depict dogs in human situations, including playing poker. An updated sketch of dogs playing cards was provided by Marty Bucella below. Frankly, dogs would be terrible poker players. Every time they drew good cards, they would wag their tails furiously. If the dogs drew bad cards, they would probably whine. It is always better to find the place and role best suited for a person or dog than try to embrace an unsuitable role, such as dogs playing poker.

© Martin Bucella. Used with permission.

# 3

# communicating Better

© Martin Bucella. Used with permission.

***I am pretty good about*** *letting people know when I want something. When I want to go out in the morning, for example, but the humans are still in bed, I whine. If that does not wake the adults, I growl. If that still does not work, I lick Scott's face; that almost always works.*

*Sometimes I can communicate by just lying quietly. When I think Scott may be oversleeping for our morning walk, I sometimes lie next to his face and stare at him. He usually senses something—perhaps he smells my nice dog breath—and generally opens one eye first. He sees my big brown eyes and possibly hears my tail thumping the bed. He also knows I will start licking him if he does not get up quickly. We have never been late for our walk.*

*When I am hungry or need to go out during the day, I can whine, bark, or just act antsy. Sometimes I act antsy even when I don't need to go to the bathroom but just want to go for a walk. When I act antsy, Scott gets the message. Getting what you want is all about knowing how to communicate.*

*It is important to observe what is happening before communicating or acting. When Scott or Patti put their shoes on, for example, I know they plan to go outside. No one wears shoes inside the house. When I see shoes, I run to the front door and act very excited about the prospect of going for a walk. I always assume they are putting on shoes to take me for a walk. Why else would anyone put on shoes?*

*Communicating appreciation is also really important. When Patti comes home, I jump for joy and cannot stop wagging my tail. I want her to know how much I missed her. She appreciates my affection and responds with pats and hugs, which I love almost as much as treats. Being nice to people generates far more positive responses than other behaviors.*

*For dogs, most communication is nonverbal, although we sometimes bark for effect. I know how another dog is going to behave, like if she wants to play, by how she responds to me. If another dog ignores me when I want to play or only wants to be chased and never wants to chase me, I just find another dog to play with.*

*Some people use communication to try to change behavior. They often criticize dogs without success. If a person wants a dog like me to behave, he or she should just offer some treats. Rewards succeed where criticism fails. For example, I am wary of children and strangers. When Scott wanted me to be friendly with our neighbor Shirley's grandchildren, Jordan and Eli, he gave them some dog treats to give to me. Soon Jordan and I were playing on the beach together and Eli and I were hanging out at Shirley's.*

*It is important to communicate with others to share the joys of finding treats, sniffing new smells, meeting new playmates, conveying affection, and avoiding misunderstandings. Nonverbal communication is more important than words for dogs—and maybe people.*

\* \* \*

Communicating effectively and accurately may be the most important of all life skills. Communicating is conveying information and emotions, and it allows others to understand circumstances and situations. Without communication, there is no shared knowledge to guide decisions. The more communication, the more informed everyone is and the better the expected results from any action.

Effective communication affects all aspects of life, including personal relationships, family and child raising, happiness, and business and work. Sadie and her friend Rosie, an Australian cattle dog who was also rescued in Texas, are on to something when they openly communicate their needs and desires.

Everyone who has ever been married or lived with a partner understands the importance of communicating with his or her significant other. Defining and communicating ideas in a context the partner can relate to and understand is usually important in reaching amicable decisions.

John Grohol, a doctor of psychology, published an article about communicating with partners and spouses. His nine steps to better communication are summarized here:

1. Stop and listen.
2. Force yourself to hear.
3. Be open and honest.
4. Pay attention to nonverbal signals.
5. Stay focused on the here and now.
6. Minimize emotion when discussing big decisions.
7. Be ready to cede an argument.
8. Use humor and playfulness.
9. Communicate, don't just talk.[1]

Most personal relationship problems likely develop due to a lack of effective communication. When people don't talk to each other, how can they understand each other's actions, motivations, needs, and priorities? When a new dog does not let Sadie sniff his butt, Sadie doesn't trust him. Like dogs, maybe humans need to either learn to "sniff" each other or find another way to communicate.

Articulating appreciation, like Sadie does when Patti comes home, may be even more important in everyday life than in business. I am often surprised how some people act entitled and expect others to provide for them and serve them as needed. If friends or family are unwilling to acknowledge and express appreciation for sacrifices and assistance, it probably means one has the wrong friends and may be too easily taken advantage of.

Communication within families can be challenging, but it is critically important to personal growth, happiness, health, and future success. According to Dr. Meline Kevorkian, communicating with children is critically important to family happiness and the children's future success. She says,

It's easy to spend time with your family and not talk at all. Many parents and kids often are attached to cell phones and iPods and, although just a few feet from each other, never exchange a word. Research suggests, however, that just talking about school can have a significant impact on your child's achievement.

Remember that kids learn in homes and learn from parents who value learning. Sit down with your kids and talk about what they have learned in school and what they plan to achieve. Families who stay informed about their children's progress at school have higher-achieving children.

She also advises, "Start intimate communication early on about everything, and you have a greater chance of continuing this communication into the teen years."[2]

Despite my frequent travel schedule and workload during my long career, I never missed a teacher consultation or school meeting with my children's teachers. It was important to me and my wife to be involved with our children's education. Both of our sons went on to achieve advanced degrees and career success, and our family's emphasis on education likely provided an important contribution.

Human communication takes many forms, such as written notes or letters, phone calls, texting, posting on social media, and face-to-face verbal speech. However, communication also includes nonverbal missives. In business and in life generally, people often do not recognize that they are sending nonverbal signals. Communication would be much more effective if we all used looks and body movements, like Sadie and her friend Rosie, to deliver messages consciously and deliberately and were on the lookout for others' nonverbal messages.

Like Sadie, I am not good at hiding my feelings. When someone asks, "What's wrong?" I realize I am sending out nonverbal signals. Instead of hiding such feelings, it is usually better to be open to discussing what is troubling me.

Dogs are not good at masking feelings either. When happy, they wag their tails and show enthusiasm. Dogs seem to thrive with their transparent feelings; people would do well to develop this behavioral trait.

The importance of nonverbal communication has even been acknowledged by automation experts. Assembly line robots that work with humans are often designed with facial-feature panels including digitized eyes and mouths. The robots can be programmed to look approving when tasks are successfully completed or look questioning when a task is not done as expected. They can be programmed to appear to look at an object before picking it up, which signals nearby humans of an intended action.

 Dogs communicate with humans using their nonverbal skills. Sadie's neighbor Rosie likes to catch things like Frisbees. When she wants her owner, Rick, to throw a Frisbee on their patio, she looks at the object and then looks at Rick. She repeats as necessary, letting Rick know that she wants him to throw the Frisbee.

On the beach, Rosie likes Rick to throw balls she can fetch. When Rick puts the ball launcher in his back pocket, Rosie often jumps and tries to remove it and the ball from Rick's pocket. Rick understands exactly what Rosie is communicating.

When Rosie does not want to do something like get in the car, she lowers her head and glares. Dog walker Deeba calls it her "stink glare." Without using any words, Rosie makes it clear that she does not want to go somewhere or do something.

The importance of communication is impossible to overstate but difficult to summarize. Jack Welch, the longtime CEO of General Electric, once expressed the top three priorities for being successful in business; his number two priority was the need to communicate.[3]

At work, there are several important constituencies for a manager to communicate with, including employees, senior colleagues, and other stakeholders like investors or donors. Communicating with employees and colleagues is critical; there is only so much an individual can accomplish, even a CEO. Every organization relies on staff (and some on volunteers) to implement plans and programs. At Center America and at Investa, where I was brought in as CEO, the companies were rapidly losing money. We needed to introduce many changes, but the employees also needed to buy into them, or the desired changes would not be successfully implemented. At both companies, we started a CEO call once a month. I stood in front of the employees with branch offices connected by video or telephone, talked about what the company was doing and why, and then answered questions. Often, department heads discussed their initiatives and challenges. Employees participated fully and soon realized they played an important role in making sure the company succeeded.

Many companies and organizations use similar town hall meetings with employees, but such meetings are typically infrequent. Such meetings demonstrate a concern for employees and allow a CEO to show he or she is a real person and is concerned about questions the employees may have. Regularly scheduled employee meetings with the CEO are more effective than occasional or less frequent meetings.

I learned at an early age the importance of communicating with employees. When I was young and worked in a factory many years ago, Jim Miller, the president of the company, often stopped by to ask how the employees were doing and solicit suggestions on how to improve what they did. He shared insights about how the company was performing, possible changes, and future directions. His concern and interest in each employee, including low-level assembly line workers like me, made all the workers more appreciative and willing to work harder for a leader they liked and respected.

It is critically important to communicate any proposed change and the rationale for the change. Too often leaders talk about the need for change but don't convey details or let others know what's about to happen. Meetings occur behind closed doors, conference calls are held confidentially, and consultants are retained without clear explanation to those who will be potentially affected. As a result, employees often become depressed and worry about their future. They often become distracted and distrustful. Rumors often destroy productivity and morale. Knowledge is the only clear antidote to otherwise destructive rumors.

Most communication within organizations occurs in unplanned and unstructured ways, much like Sadie unexpectedly meeting a new dog on a walk. Employees talk about work over coffee, during lunch, or between work-related projects. This informal communication is important for achieving a common understanding and sharing best practices and work experience. At Investa, despite its accumulating losses and negative cash flow, we spent $500,000 to expand an employee lounge. I believed it was essential for employees to have a nice place in the company to relax and compare notes and experiences.

One day, as I was eating lunch in the newly expanded lounge, I asked a longtime employee in the accounting services department if she knew anything about a large, old clock in the office that was not working and was gathering dust. She knew all about the history and even knew someone in the documentation department who had the winding key. Soon a group of older employees took on the responsibility of caring for it, and we had the beautiful clock restored and hung in a prominent location just outside the break room. It came to symbolize employee pride. Planning a physical workspace to facilitate employee interaction is critically important to communication and teamwork, and successfully creating this space should lead to better organizational performance.

When business conditions are most challenging, it is particularly important to recognize employees' work efforts and openly acknowledge their contributions. Employees' continued efforts are required for a company to succeed, and everyone wants to be acknowledged—just like Sadie tells Patti how much she appreciates her whenever Patti comes home.

Communication with distant offices is especially challenging in business, and nonverbal communication is difficult in such situations. Branch offices are usually connected to the home office by technology such as videoconferencing, but communication between offices is never as intimate as a face-to-face conversation within an office. For this and other reasons, I prefer a decentralized operations model for companies that service large geographic areas.

I served as president and chief operating officer of New Plan Excel Realty Trust, a well-respected NYSE-listed real estate investment trust, before it was acquired in 2006. We initially utilized a highly centrally controlled operating model. However, early in 2003, we introduced fully staffed regional offices with a full complement of professional disciplines. The overall performance of our widely dispersed properties increased dramatically as a result of the empowered new regional staff.

This experience parallels my experience in decentralizing decision-making at Plaza Properties of America, Investa, and Center America. There is a traditional Chinese saying: "The mountains are high, and the emperor is far away." Modern organizations would do well to embrace the idea that local decisions are generally best made by local people, similar to Sadie's focus on people and dogs she can see and smell.

Communications must extend to a range of interested parties, including business partners. At both Center America and Investa, we started a corporate newsletter depicting accomplishments and showcasing our key staff. This contributed to both staff and business partners feeling that they were part of a winning team. It is important to reach out to lenders, investors, and vendors and make them feel like they are part of the corporate team with a shared goal of success.

## Talking Dog for Sale

A favorite story is about a guy who saw a hand-drawn sign on the side of the road: Talking Dog for Sale. He stopped at the house ahead, knocked on the door, and asked the homeowner, "Do you really have a talking dog?"

"Yes," replied the owner. "Do you want to meet him?"

They both went to the backyard, where an undistinguished mixed-breed dog was sitting.

"Do you talk?" asked the visitor.

"Of course," the dog answered in perfect English.

"Where did you learn to talk?" asked the visitor.

"Where does anyone learn to talk?" replied the dog. "I learned from listening to others around me. I have had a great career. When the CIA discovered I could listen and talk, they had me travel around the world and sit in meetings where no one knew I could listen and then report what was being said. But I retired after seven years—seven years is a long time in dog years, and I was getting tired of all the travel."

The amazed visitor turned to the homeowner and asked, "How much do you want for this talking dog?"

"Ten dollars," replied the owner.

"Only ten dollars for a talking dog?" the visitor asked incredulously.

"Yes," replied the owner. "The dog is a lying SOB; he has never been outside the backyard."

At Investa, we started a marketing and public relations department, even though we were losing money. We wanted to communicate our story to a larger audience and felt this was an essential part of doing business. Too often, marketing efforts are curtailed when organizations seek to reduce costs, which is the opposite of what often needs to happen. It is important to let others know about an organization's successes and plans because almost everyone—investors, bankers, donors, and employees—wants to be associated with successful organizations and people.

In Sydney, I was a member of the American Club, which was recapitalized and reopened in 2010. In an effort to save money, the club did not hire a full-time marketing director. As membership waned, the club continued to reduce operating costs. Cutting costs is a short-term solution to a temporary problem; increasing revenues is eventually required for survival. Ultimately, the American Club had few expenses but insufficient revenue and was forced to close.

Today, it is increasingly important to use social media to communicate with customers and constituents. This and other books, for example, are promoted using Twitter, Facebook, and other platforms that are now considered critical for commercial success. If an author does not have an active presence on social media, for example, then book distributors, bookstores, and even publishers are less likely to support a proposed new book.

As consumers increasingly turn to digital and social media platforms for information, having presence and visibility on the internet is important to marketing almost any product. The future will be very different from the past in this fundamental regard.

Newspapers previously dominated advertising for retail stores, including department stores, in markets throughout the country and the developed world. As newspaper circulations decline, advertisers are forced to turn to digital information sources to reach customers. With data-mining techniques, retailers identify and categorize potential customers with better targeted precision than was previously available.

Recently, I listened to a presentation by an executive with a national retail chain of fashion stores. The company is implementing a system that will identify customers entering their stores using each customer's smartphone. It will determine what that customer purchased previously and text him or her sales offers on similar, potentially appealing merchandise. The company also plans to look at the customer's presence on social media and send merchandise suggestions compatible with the customer's profile. Apparently, other retailers are developing similar digital merchandising techniques to identify possible customers and match their buying profiles with merchandise offerings.

My friend Bob is always looking for a good deal. Recently, Bob proudly shared with me his new smartphone app, which alerts him every time he passes a store with something on sale. Unfortunately, his phone is constantly dinging with alerts as nearby retailers solicit Bob's patronage.

With the growth and almost universal availability of smartphones, communication is easier than it has ever been. Within seconds, almost anybody can send a text message, an email, or a message utilizing a large variety of apps such as Snapchat, Facebook, or LinkedIn to acquaintances around the world. There is no excuse not to communicate and communicate often— unless you are a dog and cannot use a smartphone.

---

## Being honest and candid is the best way to communicate bad news, coupled with a plan to fix what went wrong.

---

The need to communicate openly and frequently with owners, directors, or bosses is probably self-evident. But communicating problems and intended solutions is as important as communicating good news. Hiding bad news or trying to pretend a problem is not a problem leads to loss of credibility and distrust. Without trust, leadership cannot succeed—and neither can personal relationships or anything else.

There is a tendency in business and in life to try to cover up problems or spin mistakes to recharacterize losses as wins. Politicians spin or redefine issues regularly, and it is not surprising that people hold politicians in low regard (according to all recent national polls). Being honest and candid is the best way to communicate bad news, coupled with a plan to fix what went wrong.

At an analyst and investor presentation of Investa's listed company, Investa Office Fund, an investor asked about the fund's poorly performing investment in the Dutch Office Fund. The fund manager tried to spin the answer, indicating that the future looked good. I interrupted him and indicated the investment was a big mistake, we would not recover anytime soon, and we needed to find a way to exit the investment. The next day, we received several calls from investors indicating appreciation for the honesty, and the published analyst reports generally congratulated Investa management for their candor. The stock price increased too; honest communication usually pays good dividends.

Understanding whom one is dealing with, including his or her background, tendencies, values, and timing considerations, is critical in any important discussion or negotiation. Knowledge of the other party provides key advantages in communicating the benefits of a prospective agreement or articulating a position using language and examples most likely to be understood and embraced by the other party.

Occasionally, I ask my associates to refrain from talking when we are meeting for the first time with a prospective partner or investor. I want the partner or investor to talk so I can learn more about his or her priorities and sensitivities. You never learn things when you talk; you learn when others talk. Shakespeare had the right idea when he said, "Give every man thy ear, but few thy voice"—in other words, listen to many, but speak to a few.[4]

## chapter Takeaways

1. Nonverbal communication is important.
2. Open and honest communication is the best solution to virtually all situations.
3. Expressing appreciation is critical in life and at work.

# 4

# Living in the Moment

© Martin Bucella. Used with permission.

*I live in the moment. I like to play tug-of-war with my friend Beau, but I never think about past battles or possible future battles. Such thoughts would distract from what is happening right now. When Beau grabs a leash or a rope toy, I grab it too, and we are engaged in a real battle. If Beau is not around or is uninterested in a tug-of-war, Rosie might want to play chase, and any distractions like thinking about Beau would cause me to miss out on the resulting fun chase.*

*When I see Chewy, a big brown Labradoodle, with a stick, I decide whether or not to try to take it away. I don't think about what I would do if Chewy had a stick when he doesn't have a stick; that would waste my time and prevent me from reacting to what is happening. And I don't think about the times in the past when Chewy had a stick, because I am busy looking for treats or playing right now. Why waste time thinking about things that are already over or unlikely to happen?*

*It is good to remember certain things that help me in the present. For example, I remember when I found treats in a certain bush because I want to check that bush whenever I walk by. There could be more treats there now. Finding new treats is much more important than savoring the memory of finding treats in the past. I can't eat memories, even if I can remember things.*

*I remember which dogs are good to play with and which dogs to avoid based on past encounters. But this helps me in the present circumstances. Recalling a good chase in the past or imagining a chase in the future does not help me find someone to play with right now.*

*My memory is not that great, but I do remember key words and phrases like* go out, walk, *and* treats. *And I certainly know who takes care of me, what couches and beds are the softest, when I get fed, and who has treats—the important stuff.*

*I never worry about what* might *happen; that seems like a worthless activity and could distract me from enjoying life as it occurs. It could interfere with my naps and my focus on watching for UPS drivers and other visitors. I could even miss a dog walking by and forget to bark if I were thinking about things that were not actually happening.*

*Being present also means connecting with what is happening now. I like to look at Scott; actually, I often stare at him, and we make eye contact. That tells Scott I am present and connecting to him rather than thinking about something else.*

*In bed at night, I always start out in the middle of the bed near the foot. This affords Patti and Scott lots of room. But as the night progresses, I often move and lie against Patti or Scott. This is my way of connecting to them at the moment. It feels good to be connected, even if Scott falls out of bed sometimes as he tries to give me room.*

\* \* \*

From the moment after we are born until we die, we all have a past, a present, and a future. In my experience, most people and organizations focus on the present and the future, but each has individual priorities and preferences. How these preferences are used and prioritized affects the happiness of the individuals and the success of organizations.

I have met many people who seem more focused on the past. They enjoy sharing stories from when they were younger and telling tales of long ago. Sometimes these are older people who have more past than future and who may long for the past and the familiar. Sometimes they are people whose memories of the past are better than their current circumstances. Maybe their well-paying job was eliminated and now they are struggling. Maybe their health is not as good as it was, or perhaps their aspirations were never realized and it is easier to recall the days when their dreams were real and their hopes were not limited by the ensuing reality.

It's okay to recall good memories; I have wonderful memories of being the father to my young sons when they were growing up. But living in the past causes current opportunities to be missed and future options to be lost. The more time one spends in the past, the less time one has for the present and the future.

Sometimes people search the past to recount previous lessons learned in the context of understanding the present. Perhaps they are trying to comprehend what is new and unexperienced by recalling prior experiences. Looking to the past for clues is different and more beneficial than dwelling in the past.

I also think that people's memories of the past are often more positive than past experiences actually were. This nostalgia often revolves around memories and favorable experiences with others and results in one's sense of social support and connection. Nostalgia is often triggered by current or recent negative experiences and feelings and can serve as a coping mechanism.

BJ (short for Beetlejuice) is a large black Labrador retriever that lives nearby with David. BJ is certified as a comfort dog and is permitted to ride in passenger cabins on airlines. One time, David bought BJ and himself first-class seats to Hawaii; they were sitting in their seats as other passengers boarded. A young boy asked if he could pet BJ; David said yes. After petting the dog, the boy turned to his mother and asked, "If a dog can fly first class, why can't I fly first class?"

Living in the past can provide psychological comfort and escape from seemingly less desirable present circumstances. But it can also be delusional and can prevent one from recognizing and adjusting to current circumstances and opportunities.

Alternatively, living in a past filled with negative experiences and bad memories can be depressing and reinforce negative feelings and a negative outlook. Some people seem to dwell on perceived past injustices, slights, or unfair treatment. This preoccupation with the past can translate into negativity, unhappiness, and poor expectations for the future.

Negative memories may be particularly burdensome for couples who have divorced. When we first marry and are in love, we believe the marriage will last forever. We embrace the "until death do us part" vow that is typical of a wedding ceremony. When things do not work out as planned, partners often blame each other and sometimes continue to dwell on their anger and hard feelings long after the divorce is finalized. We all need to move on, find a new relationship or life situation, and embrace a more positive future.

For organizations, living in the past can be catastrophic. Life and businesses change, and those whose actions mirror the past miss the opportunity to stay current and competitive. It's like driving a car while looking only in the rearview mirror.

In contrast to focusing on the past, living in the present offers significant benefits. If one is not looking at the present, he or she will miss the many wonderful things that happen every day and will not deal effectively with the not-so-wonderful things that occur on occasion. For people, living in the present means being connected to others in real time. It means creating and sustaining meaningful relationships, parenting children who live in the present, making and supporting friends, and being supported by friends. It is all about connecting and caring.

Being in the present makes one more aware of current reality and better able to respond to it. Understanding and responding to one's present circumstances contributes to defining one's future. Buddha advised, "Do not dwell in the past, do not dream of the future, concentrate the mind on the present moment."[1] Henry David Thoreau concurred: "You must live in the present, launch yourself on every wave, find your eternity in each moment."[2]

Psychologist Jay Dixit says, "Life unfolds in the present. But so often we let the present slip away, allowing time to rush past unobserved and unseized and squandering the precious seconds of our lives as we worry about the future and ruminate about what's past." Living in the present is also called *mindfulness* in Buddhist teaching. According to Dixit, who cites past studies, "Cultivating a nonjudgmental awareness of the present bestows a host of benefits. Mindfulness reduces stress, boosts immune functioning, reduces chronic pain, lowers blood pressure, and helps patients cope with cancer. . . . Mindful people are happier, more exuberant, more empathetic, and more secure. They have higher self-esteem and are more accepting of their own weaknesses."

Dixit lists six steps to living in the moment:

1. To improve your performance, stop thinking about it.
2. To avoid worrying about the future, focus on the present.
3. If you want a future with your significant other, inhabit the present.
4. To make the most of time, lose track of it.
5. If something is bothering you, move toward it rather than away from it.
6. Know that you don't know.[3]

Mindfulness appears to have originated with the writings of Buddha. The last Buddha wrote in the Pali language, and the Pali word *sati* has been loosely translated as "to remember, memory, thoughtfulness."[4] It is generally used today in yoga and in Buddha's teaching of complete focus and attention on what is happening in the moment.

Mindfulness has many benefits, including being more connected in relationships. When Sadie locks eyes with me, she is connecting. Similar connections happen in the human world.

Some people struggle with the present. Many suffer from stress, anxiety, or depression. My neighbor and renowned psychologist Pam Laidlaw suggests such people obtain professional help and look to the past to understand what prior conditions and circumstances could be contributing to problems in the present. She also suggests humor as a universal remedy to help improve one's outlook.

As beneficial as living in the present can be, an awareness and appreciation of the future is important for people and organizations. Dogs live in the present, but people and organizations need to anticipate the future if they are to realize success.

As clear as this concept seems, I have met many executives who rarely change organizational structure and operations, do not regularly update technology, and retain loyal but no longer competent staff. When I worked at the Hahn Company many years ago, we retained many project development staff members long after the number of our development projects was greatly diminished. We remembered the past times of many projects and hoped those days would return. These attitudes cause organizations to decline as they lose business and support to others more focused on the present and the future.

I have lived most of my life in the future, unlike Sadie. I have always yearned to improve myself, to learn as much as I can every day, to work harder and smarter than others, and to generally position myself for future opportunities. I am never content with where I am or what I know. This has served me well in life and in my career. When I was eighteen years old, I worked on a factory assembly line; when I was forty years old, I was a CEO. Being focused and cognizant of trends and future directions leads to being well positioned to take advantage when future opportunities become available. But I am also aware of the present and the joys and opportunities afforded by being connected in the moment.

Organizations that focus on the future are similarly better positioned to succeed as their market evolves and conditions change. Driving by looking in the rearview mirror or not driving at all—just sitting in the car and not going anywhere—are not helpful strategies for organizations or people.

Organizations must operate in the present until the future arrives. That means taking care of current customers with current needs, leading and

Joan's dog, Spartan, is a mixed Lab like Sadie. He likes to ride in the front seat next to Joan when she is driving her car. Whenever Joan drives somewhere, Spartan begs to go with her. One time, Joan and Spartan drove into an HOV highway entrance lane and were stopped by a police officer for not having a second passenger. Joan forgot for the moment that Spartan was a dog and not a person. (Spartan probably did not recognize the difference either.) Joan pleaded with the policeman that Spartan was the second passenger, and her use of the HOV lane was legal, but unfortunately the officer was not a dog owner and gave Joan a ticket.

inspiring existing employees, and competing with others who exist right now. The path to the future must go through the present.

Sadie lives in the present; people and companies must recognize and connect with the present while keeping an eye on the future. Unlike dogs, people can think ahead and identify how conditions may change and how best to respond. But always thinking in future tense will lead to missing good opportunities in the present, including personal connections and deeper relationships.

### Chapter Takeaways

1. Appreciate and learn from the past.
2. Embrace and connect with the present.
3. Plan for the future.

Sadie on the beach at dawn. © Peter Steusloff. Used with permission.

# 5

# Planning Your Escape

© Martin Bucella. Used with permission.

*Humans like to create walls and fences.* *They use their fences to keep dogs like me from running free. They also seem to use fences to keep other humans from straying from the desired path. They can use chains to keep us dogs in place, but not often. I understand from Scott that they sometimes "chain humans to their desks at work," which really seems strange.*

*Maybe humans who are fenced in or chained up should do what every reputable dog does: plan an escape to a better place. I can think of several ways to escape one's confines. The easiest is to wait for someone to open the gate and then make a run for it. Almost all dogs are quicker than human fence people.*

*If the "run through the gate plan" is not successful, there are other options, and I always have other plans in case the first attempt fails. First, I would walk the fence line and look for gaps. Sometimes, one fence does not completely link to an adjacent fence, which provides an opportunity. Scott lets me out in the side yard; he thinks his fence is solid. But I found a gap at the very end where his fence ends and his neighbor Tanya's fence begins. He can't see the space between the fences, but when I want to escape to the front yard, I can go through the hidden gap.*

*Another option is to find a way to open the gate by myself. My neighbors Klaus and Dagmar used to have a golden retriever named Charlie. Whenever they had a party, they would lock her in the bedroom. The bedroom door had a door handle, and simply pushing against the door would not cause it to open. But Charlie was a smart dog and soon learned to push the handle down and pull the door open at the same time. She never missed a party.*

*If there is no gap in the fence, and the gate cannot be opened, it is possible to go over or under the fence. There is a German shepherd who comes to Markim Pet Resort on occasion. He can actually climb the fence and get to the other side. For me, going over is not a good option. It is important to know one's limitations, and I am just not a high jumper or climber.*

*So the final option is to dig under the fence. Some dogs are better diggers than others, but we can all dig if we try.*

*Everyone needs a plan for after the escape. Once the owner realizes the gap exists in the fence or understands that someone knows how to open the door, don't expect many future opportunities. Everyone needs to be prepared unless he or she wants to go back to sniffing grass all day in an enclosure.*

* * *

The Chinese philosopher Confucius said about 2,500 years ago, "Success depends on previous preparation, and without such preparation, there is sure to be failure." Everyone needs to be prepared when opportunities become available to escape to a better place. Over time, carefully observe and determine conditions and patterns before planning a move.

One will never succeed unless one is prepared when opportunities arise. Hall of Fame basketball coach Roy Williams and other notable leaders (including former New York City mayor Michael Bloomberg) have repeated the phrase, "The harder you work, the luckier you get." Success in life is usually greatly influenced by being prepared for future opportunities. And then when the opportunity occurs, someone who is prepared will be able to

Patti's dog, Sophie, a fourteen-year-old minia-ture pinscher mix, is blocked from exiting her patio by a big, latched gate. She is a tiny dog confronted by a tall gate. But Sophie is a de-termined little dog who is persistent when she wants something, and she likes to go out front to visit neighbors and play. She has learned that if she jumps against the gate, the latch will open, and she can leave. It took Patti a long time to figure out how little Sophie could open the latch.

advance. Dogs (and people) who just hang out in the yard, sniff the grass, and dream of an open gate and the opportunities available elsewhere will never make it to bigger pastures.

The history of humans escaping physical enclosures is not encouraging for someone fenced in, but there are examples of successful escapes. The greatest historical escapes generally involve a disguise, digging tunnels, or having inside help. Mary, Queen of Scots, was imprisoned in 1567 by Queen Elizabeth in remote Loch Leven Castle. First, she dressed as a laundress and tried to exit but was unsuccessful. Subsequently, she befriended an orphan who knew hidden passages to aid her escape. Once outside the castle walls, she took a boat and then mounted a stolen horse and rode away.

In 1597, a Jesuit priest, John Gerard, was able to remove the stones from around his door in the Tower of London, sneak past the guards, lower him-self with a rope into a waiting boat that had been arranged by a friendly Tower superintendent, and speed away. This was one of the few successful escapes from the Tower of London.

The famous Italian lover Casanova was imprisoned in Leads Prison. He found an iron bar, however, and managed to dig a tunnel with a fellow inmate.

Henry Brown, a runaway slave, was shipped in a box from North Caro-lina to Pennsylvania in 1849. Fortunately, the post office did not lose the package and delivered it on time, allowing Brown to survive the long journey.

In World War II, seventy-six prisoners of war in Germany's Stalag Luft III managed to dig tunnels and escape, although most were recaptured and killed on Hitler's orders.

 Angel is a bearded collie, or "beardie." Like most beardies, Angel likes to be with her family and does not enjoy being alone. She is also highly intelligent. When her owners, Gary and Cecy, went to Europe on a holiday, they hired a dog sitter to care for Angel. The dog sitter left Angel in the fenced backyard one day. Angel soon tired of being alone, and when no one responded to her barks at the back door, she dug under the fence and proceeded to the front door, where she waited for someone to let her in. When Gary checked his webcam on the internet from Paris, he was surprised to see Angel waiting patiently by the front door. He quickly called the dog sitter, and soon Angel was inside enjoying company and her favorite couch.

In 1949, the Dalai Lama XIV dressed as a worker and mingled with a Tibetan crowd gathered outside as the Chinese Communist Army entered his palace. He then proceeded to take a boat and safely leave Tibet.

Over time, many East Germans escaped to the West despite the Berlin Wall. Some tunneled under the wall, most were hidden in cars passing through checkpoints, and at least one couple made a hot air balloon and flew over the wall. Unfortunately, most who tried to escape did not succeed.

Humans may have a better chance of escaping psychological or metaphoric walls than physical confinements. In the human world, the path to a better life traditionally has been through education. Using published data from the US Bureau of Labor Statistics, on average, the more education someone has, the greater his or her level of income will be. Someone with a high school education earns an average of $37,000 per year compared to $61,000 for someone with a bachelor's degree and $95,500 for someone with a professional degree.[1] This translates into $1 million in additional income during a working lifetime for someone with a bachelor's degree compared to someone with a high school diploma.[2]

In the peak of the recession in early 2010, the US unemployment rate for workers with less than a high school degree was 15.8 percent compared with 5.0 percent for college graduates.[3] Not only do college graduates make more money, but they also are more likely to be employed even in challenging economic times.

---

**Preparing to escape situations that limit potential and access to opportunities almost always includes securing a good education.**

---

Education appears to be an essential key to better income, employment, self-image, happiness, and access to a better quality of life. Studies have generally shown that people with more education earn more income, have better-perceived labor status, and have a higher probability of being employed. These conditions appear to lead to greater self-confidence and better self-esteem. Thus, indirectly, education contributes to people's happiness. A recent study supports the thesis that people with more education are happier than those with less education, even when controlling for socioeconomic variables such as income.[4]

Preparing to escape situations that limit potential and access to better opportunities almost always includes securing a good education. Human preparation begins with school.

There is a trend for students at universities to pursue studies that train them for specific future careers. There is a counterargument, however, that suggests a broad liberal arts education produces a better-rounded graduate who may be better able to change jobs and careers as specialized jobs are replaced by machines in the future. I agree with the book *In Defense of a Liberal Education*, by Fareed Zakaria, which argues the need for a liberal arts education due to changing workplace demands, the possibility that specialized jobs may be replaced, and the need for critical thinking and problem solving unrelated to specialized training.[5]

Leaders in societies around the world have typically agreed on the importance of education in securing a better life. South African prime minister and Nobel Prize recipient Nelson Mandela said, "Education is the most powerful weapon which you can use to change the world."[6] T. S. Eliot, the acclaimed writer, saw education as a means to escape to a better life: "It is a fact that part of the function of education is to help us escape."[7]

The pace of social and economic change appears to be accelerating. Many existing jobs will be eliminated in the future, replaced due to advances in automation, robots, and artificial intelligence. Having a broader education and knowledge base as well as being flexible and opportunistic will be critical, especially for young people navigating careers buffeted by change.

Unrelated to their jobs and economic well-being, some people are emotionally trapped or confined by existing relationships and life situations. They may need to plan an escape to a better life. That escape may require a change in circumstances, a change in location, or a change in relationships. Staying in a captive situation deprives one of the future and hope of a better life.

Sometimes life and relationships are good, but change happens. In time, what was once good may no longer be so good. With professional help, it may be possible to return to "good," but it is not always possible to recapture what was had and then lost.

Beverly Flaxington wrote an article in *Psychology Today* titled "Feeling Stuck in the Relationship." She says,

> When you are miserable in your relationship but can't seem to let go of it, you will start to feel stuck in a flawed relationship. . . . You don't need anyone's permission to leave. You know that your relationship is flawed if:
>
> - You feel unhappy and worn out by your relationship
> - You feel happier away from your partner
> - You feel like you are talking to a wall
> - You feel controlled or patronized
> - You feel restrained or suffocated by your relationship
> - You spend all your free time worrying about the relationship
> - You have no voice, no opinion or rights
> - You don't feel valued or appreciated enough
> - You always end up at fault in every situation
> - You don't seem to have time for friends, family, or yourself
> - You have been verbally attacked or put down by your partner
> - You have been cheated on, threatened, or abused
>
> Oftentimes we feel that too much has been invested into a relationship to let it fail, so even when things don't seem to work any longer, we don't let go. . . . Why chain yourself to a sinking ship when you still have a chance to jump?

But she also cautions, "Remember that ups and downs will happen along the way . . . Do you want to work on your relationship or terminate it?" If the answer is to terminate, she says, "One critical mistake that everyone seems to make when dealing with change is waiting too long."[8]

Sometimes inertia prevents someone from acting to secure an improved life or a better job. A well-known and pertinent saying advises, "The secret of getting ahead is getting started."⁹ Too often, people delay taking action, which leads to further inaction.

Escaping to a better work and financial life often requires a willingness to change careers when market conditions change. My grandfather was trained as a telegraph operator, like his father. With the introduction of the telephone, however, there were no longer jobs available for telegraph operators, so my grandfather studied and became an accountant. Changing careers was not easy for him; he had assumed he would always be a telegraph operator like his father. But by studying to be an accountant, he was able to find a job with a railroad during the Great Depression and provide for his family.

Too often, people who follow their parents' career paths and initially make good wages seem unable to adjust when their services are no longer valued. Many autoworkers were unable to develop new skills when they lost their jobs due to cutbacks in the workforce for carmakers. Typically, their parents were autoworkers, and they assumed the same career would provide them with the same benefits and opportunities that their parents enjoyed.

---

## Escaping to a better life also requires a willingness to change careers.

---

Several years ago, I visited Ironwood, Michigan, which is located in the Upper Peninsula. The town's population peaked in 1920, but notable declines occurred subsequently as iron ore mines closed and were not replaced by other employers.

Mining was profitable in the mid-to-late 1800s and early 1900s. When the mines eventually closed, many residents of mining towns remained despite a lack of work, perhaps hoping the mines would reopen someday and restore good wages and plentiful jobs. The mines did not reopen, and those who did not change careers and geographic locations typically saw their standard of living drop significantly. Eventually, many towns declined, and some became ghost towns as younger people left and older people died.

The experience of mining in Michigan is similar to the trends in the coal industry. Every election year, politicians visit coal-producing states and proclaim support for more coal-mining jobs. I have been in rural West Virginia and Kentucky and witnessed the poverty associated with the decline of the coal industry. Unfortunately, the politicians are not being truthful; the lost coal jobs are never coming back.

Coal mining has been declining steadily since 1920. At one time coal mining accounted for about 785,000 jobs in the United States, or almost 2 percent of employment. Now, coal mining employs around 80,000 miners, according to one source, and maybe even fewer than 70,000, according to another, more recent estimate.[10] The two biggest coal-employment states, West Virginia and Kentucky, employ about 20,000 and 13,000 miners, respectively.

Natural gas is abundant and less expensive to use than coal. It is also cleaner and healthier than burning coal. There is mixed research on whether federal regulations have contributed to the loss of coal jobs, but clearly coal is in a long-term decline, regardless of regulations.

By contrast, the solar panel industry is growing rapidly and now employs about 260,000 workers.[11] Continued high levels of growth are anticipated due to the lower cost of solar panels, better technology, and favorable economics of using solar energy in many states. Ironically, the Kentucky Coal Mining Museum in Benham, Kentucky, recently installed solar panels to reduce its energy costs.

So why don't the unemployed coal miners change jobs and take advantage of solar panel job growth and availability? Perhaps relocation and retraining is not attractive to some, or possibly they are waiting for the politicians to deliver the promised new coal industry jobs. For those waiting for politicians to deliver jobs, they should learn from their counterparts in Michigan, who have been waiting for decades.

Jobs are often more plentiful in some geographic areas than in others. The northeast region of the United States was the center of textile manufacturing from the 1700s to the late 1800s. Beginning about 1880, textile mills began to relocate to the South, especially North Carolina. Unemployment rose in New England as factory work shifted. Unless textile workers in New England relocated, they either had to change careers or remain unemployed; relatively few relocated.

When I was a student at the University of North Carolina in the early 1970s, manufacturers' clothing outlet stores could be found throughout the state, especially in the central Piedmont area. Textile factories dotted the landscape and provided employment to many. By the 1990s, however, textile manufacturing migrated again in search of low-cost labor. Mills in the South closed, and new mills opened in Asia and, to a lesser extent, Latin America. This time, there was not much opportunity to relocate from

Greensboro to Shanghai, China, for example; the only option for most unemployed workers was to change careers.

My grandfather, the newly minted accountant, did secure a job with
the Burlington Railroad, but he had to move his family from the small
town of Hamburg, Arkansas, to the big cities of Detroit, Michigan, and
then Chicago, Illinois. And I had to relocate my family from Chicago to
San Diego, California, and subsequently to Houston, Texas, to secure better
employment during my career. Relocation is often required to secure better
employment options and escape more limited opportunities.

It is a common belief that the best jobs are in the United States, but this is
not necessarily correct in all cases. Today there are nine million nonmilitary
Americans living abroad.[12] Many are living in foreign countries because of
favorable employment opportunities. The twentieth century was arguably
the American century, but the twenty-first century may be more diffused
and global in providing quality jobs. People who restrict themselves to a
single geographic area, including a single country, may miss out on better options for work and life. Instead of *New-York Tribune* founder Horace
Greeley's famous quote from the nineteenth century, "Go West, young man,"
perhaps the new motto should be, "Look East, West, North, and South,
young people, before choosing where to go."

Seeking better opportunities can be done within an organization or
elsewhere. If someone has a dead-end job with a company, searching for a
better job within the organization is often a first step. Understanding what
others do at work and acquiring skills to take on greater responsibility is
important. Just going to work every day and doing your job is not a prescription for advancement.

I joined the Hahn Company in 1983 as vice president of market research.
It was a specific role with no clear upward path. However, no one at the
company had reliable cash flow models, and I had good financial skills.
I volunteered to develop financial forecasts for the company, and soon I was
also responsible for financial modeling. It helped that I became friends with
Mike Heiken, our controller, and Mike and I ran together at lunchtime. On
almost every run, I queried Mike about accounting and financial models,
and he shared his considerable knowledge. Effectively, he became my accounting instructor.

Subsequently, my staff developed a model to predict how new shopping
center developments would perform after opening. It was not part of my job
description, but I saw a need for this information. I was then promoted to

head of new developments and acquisitions, in part because of my ability to predict financial success or loss of proposed new investments and the financial skills I had developed. Finally, I became chief operating officer and acting chief executive officer, responsible for the entire company.

When a company or organization is not expanding, and the workforce is stable, there are fewer opportunities to advance. It is always more advantageous to be part of an expanding company than one that is stable or contracting. If one finds him- or herself trapped in a job in a company that offers no promotional opportunities, the best option is usually to look elsewhere.

In my experience, almost all jobs are obtained through personal contacts and introductions. If an employee has impressed colleagues and business associates with the quality of his or her work and work ethic, he or she can use those contacts to find a better position. I have hired hundreds of people in my career, but I do not recall ever hiring anyone based on an unsolicited résumé and letter. I think I am pretty typical. I rely on reputation and the recommendations of people I know and trust.

I feel sorry for unemployed workers who sit at home or in temporary offices, sending out scores of résumés and cover letters to people they do not know in search of a good job. This is usually a losing strategy, based on my experience.

There is a recent trend of asking job applicants to undertake tasks or assignments as part of the job interview process. Sometimes résumés are not even provided or evaluated. The theory is that how a prospective employee performs on a work-related assignment is more important than his or her prior experience, which may have been exaggerated on a résumé.

There are so many examples of people being constrained by lack of opportunity, but many do not appear willing to make the changes necessary to escape their confines and seek a better life elsewhere. There appear to be several reasons for inaction when action is logically beneficial. A few reasons or excuses for inaction include the following:

1. People are comfortable with the status quo. Even if they are constrained by disadvantages and limited opportunities, many people enjoy having familiar surroundings, nearby friends and family, and local knowledge. They sacrifice potentially better economic status and income for the comfort of home.
2. Many jobs are in areas with high housing and living costs. Even if a better job and income are available, the economic benefit may be offset by higher costs of living, especially housing.

3. People fear failure. One theory suggests the sting of failure may exceed the likely benefits of success. Failure in some cultures is particularly unforgiving. A business failure in Australia appears far more hurtful to one's career there than a failure in the United States, for example.

4. People fear the unknown. It was courageous for my small-town Arkansas grandparents to pack up their family and move to a big city in the North during the Great Depression. Many people would have been too afraid to move to such a different place and culture despite the dire economic circumstances at home.

5. Some cultures are more accepting of their current lifestyle and economic status. If one's friends and neighbors are comfortable with their status and lifestyle, there is less urgency to improve one's economic status. If such behavior is accompanied by excuses or blame ("the government or big business is the reason I do not have a good job"), there is less perceived incentive to escape.

In life, everyone will be confronted by obstacles and fences. People can accept their confinement and live their lives constrained by enclosures—they can even blame others for their misfortune—but that will not make the fences disappear. If someone wants a better alternative, he or she should plan carefully, be prepared, and take advantage of the opportunities that arise. Otherwise, he or she will remain captive, chained to his or her desk, sniffing the same grass over and over for an entire career or life.

### Chapter Takeaways

1. If someone feels fenced in or chained to a job or life situation, it's time to act.
2. Blaming others or circumstances will not solve the problem.
3. Failure to act will likely result in a life of confinement.

# 6

# Avoiding Certain Dogs

GRRR

© Martin Bucella. Used with permission.

***I meet a lot of dogs on the beach in the morning.*** *Some dogs are fun and want to play; we chase each other up and down the beach until we are exhausted. Cooper is like this.*

*Chewy is a puppy with lots of energy; he does not know when to stop. Sometimes we play, but when I tire of his nonstop action, I just tell him to chase Rosie, and he is off and running. Sometimes, you have to divert a dog's attention when he or she is being irritating.*

*Some dogs are just mean. There is a big, black dog around the corner that growls and bares his teeth when I look at him from across the street. I feel sorry for angry dogs because they generally have issues at home.*

*Some dogs are usually nice but become unfriendly in certain situations. Rosie, for example, is aggressive only when she is leashed or protecting a favorite toy or bone. Mira, a German shepherd, can be friendly and playful, but when she gets too excited, she bites or chews on other dogs' necks without realizing she is hurting them.*

*Dogs are, by nature, loving animals. If a dog misbehaves, something is not right, but the dog can be trained to correct unacceptable behavior. Almost all the dogs I know have been to a trainer. I know some dogs that need medications to calm down.*

*It's important to be nice to new dogs and dogs you do not know well. Be nice to the dogs you pass on the street, because you will almost certainly pass them again on the way back.*

*Sometimes I meet a puppy like Titan, a Bernese mountain dog who lives nearby. I played with Titan even when he was a young pup, although he could be a pain because he was slow and not that coordinated. Now Titan is more than twice as big as me, and we still play, but I am careful not to let him catch me, because he is still a bit clumsy—and he is also really big.*

*Dogs often change as they grow up. Puppies can be irritating and troublesome. Cooper, a miniature Goldendoodle who lives around the corner, and Cannoli, an Australian shepherd who lives a block away, have so much energy, they cannot stop jumping and wanting to play, even when I do not encourage them. I know they will eventually calm down. I just have to be patient.*

*Dogs know which dogs to avoid. We sense when a dog is unfriendly or wants to be assertive. We recognize the telltale signs when the hair on the back rises or ears fold backward. We also sense when a dog is hiding aggression beneath the surface. In contrast, we know when a dog is friendly by the wag of his or her tail and the relaxed, curious sniff. When we encounter a potentially aggressive alpha dog, we just acknowledge the other dog and let him or her know we don't intend to challenge or confront.*

\* \* \*

We all meet many different people in life and business. In both, one usually tries to associate with friends, colleagues, and partners who have good values and ethics as well as with mentors and people who can help us. Whom one chooses to associate with will greatly influence his or her life and career.

Important associations and values start at an early age. There have been studies that suggest a person's performance in school can be predicted by the

 Sometimes little dogs like to think they are powerful alpha dogs—or at least they appear to try to overcompensate for their short stature. They have a "Marshall complex." Marshall, a white toy shih tzu, tries to boss all the bigger dogs on the beach. He goes toe to toe with big Labrador retrievers like Riley and Bailey. Bhavi is also a shih tzu with a pushy demeanor. When Marshall and Bhavi were in dog training together, it must have been quite a challenge. When either tries to act bossy with Sadie, she ignores them. When they see they aren't getting attention, they move on.

neighborhood (or postal code) he or she lives in.[1] This is likely due to many factors, including economic status, but it may also reflect parents deliberately moving to neighborhoods with good schools and neighbors who similarly value access to quality education. I suspect it is also due to students being surrounded by contemporaries who value educational achievement more than other objectives. Making sure a child's friends have desirable values and ethics begins a long-term socialization process that will influence his or her ultimate success.

When my wife and I moved to the Chicago area from the Washington, DC, area, we chose Evanston as a place to live and start a family. We were attracted to the good schools, the presence of Northwestern University, and the diversity of the community. Our first child was born in Evanston, and we enjoyed making good friends with neighbors who were supportive and generally shared our values.

When we moved to Houston, we chose a house in the Memorial Villages, which also offered good public schools and an engaged community of neighbors. My wife was elected to the local city council and served on the parent-teacher association (PTA), and our sons received an excellent education. Unfortunately for me, the house was nowhere near my job, but finding the right neighborhood and schools was more important than my commuting distance.

I think everyone who has worked for a while and been successful can identify a mentor who was important in shaping his or her life. We can also name the friends who gave us support when needed and reinforced good value systems and behavioral standards. When selecting a place to work or live, it is important to understand the values and ethics of those whom one will work or spend time with. If other people do not share your aspirational goals and behavioral norms and standards, find another organization or move to another neighborhood because otherwise life will be less enjoyable and progress will be hindered.

## Important associations and values start at an early age.

When we associate with people who are good influences, they tend to pull us up. Their examples, which we often see and seek to emulate, make us better, happier, and more successful. We should all strive to be a good influence on others.

In contrast, bad influences tend to drag us down. Internist Dr. Alex Lickerman warns of the negative effects of associating with bad influences: "Some people are simply toxic, complaining constantly, gossiping mercilessly, even purposely sabotaging others. . . . We should avoid such people as best we can."[2]

Even if someone is not toxic, his or her negativity can adversely affect our outlook and actions. The website PairedLife lists ten types of people to stay away from. These are people who take the following negative actions:

1. Make fun of you
2. Bully or dominate you
3. Take you for granted
4. Are always complaining
5. Have broken your heart
6. Have lied, betrayed, or cheated you
7. Find faults in you regularly
8. Constantly try to change you
9. Are not trustworthy
10. Have given you bad memories[3]

We can likely identify those who would have led us down a wrong path had we associated with them more closely. Carefully choosing which people to surround oneself with—friends, partners, or colleagues—and which people *not* to associate with will significantly influence one's future happiness and success.

Sometimes, it is necessary to avoid people (or dogs) for circumstantial reasons even if they are friendly and nice. For example, it is probably a good idea to not spend too much time alone with the recently divorced, attractive neighbor if one wants to sustain his or her marriage.

When I lived in Philadelphia, Pennsylvania, before I was married, I asked my assistant, Stephanie, about a single girl in the office. Stephanie told me Mary's father was a big shot in the mafia, and if I messed with her, I would wind up stuffed in a barrel in south Philadelphia. I thought Stephanie was joking until I noticed local police were finding guys stuffed in barrels regularly. Eventually, I decided not to pursue Mary and risk the barrel.

A favorite saying of mine is "Be nice to the people you pass climbing the ladder of success, because you will see the same people on your way down the ladder later." A related saying is "Hold the ladder steady for your colleagues who are ascending because you will need someone to hold the ladder for you when you are ready to climb higher."

In managing organizations, whenever an employee seeks to advance by making another employee look bad, it is almost always better to confront the one who seeks to advance at the expense of another and terminate him or her if that behavior continues. Someone who verbally shoots another in the back almost always suffers more than the person he or she intended to shoot. That is because the damage to the reputation of the shooter is generally greater than the damage done to the person shot.

Sometimes people change as their circumstances change. Employees who were formerly good teammates may change after they are promoted and given greater responsibilities. They can become more authoritarian and dictatorial, departing from the teamwork culture that led to their original success. Unfortunately, this happens more often than it should. In part, it represents the well-known "Peter Principle," articulated by educator Dr. Lawrence Peter in his book of the same name published in 1969, which describes employees who are promoted for past accomplishments but lack higher-level leadership and management abilities.[4] It also represents a psychological condition I often see but cannot explain.

Treating everyone with respect and consideration builds successful working relationships and is a key element in team performance. One never knows where a colleague or associate may go; a junior assistant today may be an important client tomorrow.

Honesty is the basic building block for any relationship. If someone is dishonest, move on. No exceptions. No excuses. Buddha advised words to the effect, "Three things cannot be long hidden: the sun, the moon, and the truth."[5] In my experience, the truth always emerges.

The same is true in business. When corporate executives are dishonest, the company likely will not be successful over time. The truth will emerge, and the company's reputation will be tarnished forever.

When I was much younger, I considered trading my American car for a used Mercedes diesel car. I thought it would be cool to own a Mercedes, but when I test-drove the diesel, it was clear the car was noisy, shook with vibrations, and belched odious exhaust. I passed on the opportunity.

Years later, Volkswagen (VW) announced it had a new diesel car that was quiet, obtained excellent mileage using lower-cost diesel fuel, and discharged minimal pollution. Unfortunately, we now know it was not true. In an effort to increase profits, VW engineers used software to falsify the pollution levels coming from their diesel cars. As a result, millions of cars were sold to unsuspecting buyers who overpaid, believing their cars provided excellent performance without degrading the environment. It will be difficult for Volkswagen to recapture its previously favorable reputation.

Another company, Toshiba Corporation, one of Japan's leading companies, misstated its profits by $1.2 billion over several years, according to an independent report commissioned by the board of directors in 2015. The report indicated that "lax controls" and a top-down corporate culture "under

Caesar, a retriever mix, is a rescue dog from Mexico and was particularly difficult when Cynthia adopted him. Our neighbor Tom used to tell Cynthia that the immigration officials were looking for Caesar so they could deport him for bad behavior. But Caesar had a good heart. One day, a baby seal was stranded on the beach nearby, and Caesar ran up to the pup and whined and softly barked in a tone similar to the baby seal's barking. Then Caesar gently nudged the pup back into the water, and the pup swam away safely. Even if a dog causes problems early in life, he or she can develop into a good dog with time, if given the opportunity. The same is true with people.

which it was impossible to go against the intentions of superiors" were key problems with Toshiba's corporate culture.[6]

Usually when scandals occur, they occur in an environment of lax ethics, profit seeking at the expense of disclosure, and tolerance for those who perform by breaking rules. Misdeeds by employees usually do not occur unless tolerated and encouraged by corporate leadership.

Advisors and consultants can be helpful when plotting a course forward—or they can be expensive distractions. There are some "dogs" to avoid when engaging other professionals, choosing friends and colleagues, and even evaluating investment opportunities. These include the following:

- Lawyers who are more focused on fees than results. Some lawyers seem to relish finding legal problems that must be researched thoroughly before proceeding, whereas others are more focused on finding solutions. Lawyers who only look for problems are like dogs that dig for the sake of digging without getting anywhere.
- Accountants who only see problems and say no. These are like old dogs that are set in their ways and stress out whenever the path deviates from the usual route. Also avoid accountants who say yes when it defies common sense. They are like dogs that just want to please regardless of what is happening.
- Investment bankers who are paid only if a deal happens, even when sometimes the best outcome is no deal. They are similar to dogs that are unfriendly unless constantly bribed with treats.
- Financial consultants and advisors who are paid high commissions on transactions. It is especially egregious for consultants to promote funds that pay them high initial or annual fees and charges.
- Investments that seem too good to be true, such as investments that promise high rates of return in a low-interest environment. When something seems too good to be true, it usually is. Investors in Bernie Madoff's funds discovered this when they lost most of their money, and the federal government arrested Madoff in 2008 for running a Ponzi-type scheme that had lasted for decades.
- Investments that are illiquid. When one needs money, one should be able to access one's funds by selling the investment.
- Investment sponsors who cannot demonstrate a good, consistent track record in similar investments made during similar economic conditions. Ask to talk to previous investors.
- People who complain about others regularly. When one is not present, those people will probably complain about her or him as well.

- Partners who seek material gain instead of meaningful relationships. If someone is old and rich, and his or her prospective partner is young and beautiful, the young beauty may be more attracted to the old guy's (or gal's) money than his or her personality or looks. And perhaps the old guy (or gal) doesn't care about the younger partner's personality either.

It is important to always be careful about the people one chooses to associate with. That choice will likely influence one's life and career more than any other factor.

### Chapter Takeaways

1. Choose friends and colleagues carefully.
2. The people one chooses to associate with will greatly influence one's future success and happiness.
3. Honesty is the basic building block for any relationship.

*Tough day begging for treats and wagging my tail. Don't tell Scott that I'm on the couch.*

# 7

# Knowing When to Bark

© Martin Bucella. Used with permission.

**Barking is part of what I do.** *Whenever anyone comes to the door or even approaches my house, I bark—even if it is someone I know, like Juan, the gardener. It tells Scott I am doing my job, and it makes me feel good.*

*I also protect the neighborhood against any invasions by aliens or strangers. I often sit by the window overlooking the street so I can see any invaders before they reach my house. I would like to bark whenever anyone walks by on the street, but I get in trouble for barking too much. So, I have learned to bark only when someone approaches our house or when a dog walks by; it is just common courtesy to acknowledge other dogs. If the invaders ever show, I will definitely bark and warn the neighborhood.*

*All dogs bark, but some dogs bark more than others. The littlest dogs often seem to bark the most. My neighbors Bhavi and Bhodie are small shih tzu, and they bark a lot, especially when I walk by their house. When Max, a poodle, is staying with them, all three dogs bark furiously. Barking can be contagious; one starts barking, and everyone else feels the need to participate.*

*Similarly, some dogs bark just because other dogs bark. Zug, a golden retriever who lived two doors down, barked whenever Otis, a black Lab mix who lives in the house behind Zug, barked, even if Zug had no clue why Otis was barking. Just because one dog barks, it does not mean others should do the same thing.*

*Gabby, a white miniature poodle, hangs out on her balcony most days. She is almost blind but still has a good sense of smell and hearing; she barks loudly and persistently whenever I walk by. I think she is protecting her owners and house, because when she is outside her house, Gabby is pleasant; we sniff each other and nearby plants together. Never judge a dog by its bark.*

*Barking can serve as a warning, like when I see a stranger approaching my house. And barking provides protection, because no one likes to confront a barking dog. Dogs bark more when leashed than when walking off leash; we are usually protecting or warning others not to harm our companion.*

*Generally, barking is a good thing, but too much barking or dogs barking at the wrong things can really irritate people, and it is not worth it. Rosie barks at almost everyone when she is on a leash. Maybe she is afraid or anxious about being constrained by the leash, because she doesn't bark much when she is not on the leash.*

*Barking is an important form of communicating. I cannot imagine a day without barking. But knowing when to bark is key to doing my job and being rewarded.*

\* \* \*

People exhibit similar tendencies to those described above by Sadie. Although people don't bark because someone else barks, we do often mimic others. Investors often buy a stock just because other investors are buying it; it's called momentum investing. Automobile drivers often slow down when others slow down, even if there is no accident or construction. Doing something because someone else is doing it may not make sense, but it is fairly common behavior.

In personal relationships, "barking" can have a significant effect on how good or bad a relationship becomes. Frequent complaints and criticisms cause resentment and unhappiness. The abused (or barked at) partner often withdraws or, alternatively, fights back and escalates the confrontation.

Failure to discuss problems (i.e., not barking) can also lead to resentment and future confrontation. When problems are not communicated and discussed, they do not go away but rather build up. Instead of dealing with minor specific issues, problems that are not addressed become bigger, more impactful, and more difficult to resolve.

In human terms, barking that is not alerting or communicating information can be viewed as *complaining*. Psychologist Dr. Lisa Juliano warns about those who complain too much. Characteristics of chronic complainers include the following:

1. Nothing is good enough.
2. They expect the worst—or, if not the worst, disappointment.
3. They find themselves perplexed by those who seem cheery most of the time.[1]

If someone exhibits these feelings, he or she is probably complaining too much and irritating others.

Dr. Juliano divides complaints into three general categories, which I have paraphrased:

1. The person complains about poor service or product deficiencies and is often effective in registering and bringing attention to the perceived problem. This can lead to a good outcome.
2. The person is venting or getting something off her chest, which might make her feel better but does not lead to productive engagement. Constant venting without action is the same as whining.
3. The person makes ineffective complaints, usually about something he has no control over, which can be an excuse for failure or way to blame others for problems he encounters.[2]

According to Dr. Juliano, some barking or complaining is good and helpful in achieving desirable results. For example, my partner, Patti, was a school principal for several years. When a teacher misbehaved or performed poorly, Patti usually knew about it, but sometimes it came to her attention because another teacher or a parent complained. Without a complaint, addressing the behavior would have been unnecessarily delayed to the detriment of the schoolchildren. Complaints, as long as they are fair, can provide an important and timely alert—like barking.

In other situations, barking or complaining can be counterproductive and ineffective. Complaints have an important role in people's lives, but excessive complaining, venting, or unfairly blaming others for one's problems can be irritating and unproductive.

Sometimes dogs bark because they want attention. This tactic can be a good thing, like when Sadie needs to go outside and no one is noticing. But it can also be problematic. For example, Finnegan ("Finn" for short), a young boxer in the neighborhood, barks whenever his owner's telephone rings. Finn's barking intensifies as the phone rings and even after his owner, Hanna, answers the phone. The barking is so loud that Hanna can't even hear the telephone conversation until she gives Finn a treat to quiet him. Now Finn barks even more loudly without stopping every time the phone rings until he receives a treat. Giving a barking dog more attention can reward the behavior of unwanted barking. But at least Hanna can have her phone conversation!

At work, a barking employee sometimes intends to promote his or her advancement or compensation. However, beware of self-promoters. The opposite of advancing oneself through demonstrated work effort is acting as a self-promoter. These employees try to take credit for what others have helped accomplish; they talk about their success instead of the organization's success; they are individuals when teammates are needed. Successful operations are not built around people who are self-focused and are always barking to draw attention to themselves.

In business, most companies, like Investa, where I was CEO, have formal annual staff reviews. This is a key time for an employee to speak up, review accomplishments, and ask for recognition and compensation. Companies and organizations typically invite employee responses during this time, and everyone needs to take full advantage. If companies or organizations do not have a formal employee review period, they are not managing their people well. A regular formal review is an essential part of people management. A confidential employee attitude survey is also a key management tool.

Between formal review periods, it was not uncommon for an employee to ask me, "How am I doing?" or ask advice on how to move ahead. Executives and managers (including me) typically like to give advice when asked. Asking for guidance and advice highlights someone who is concerned with self-improvement and advancing his or her career by helping the organization meet its goals. These people merit watching and mentoring.

It is permissible and acceptable to ask for a raise or to be considered for a promotion. Often, an employee will ask, "What can I do to be considered for a promotion or to make more money?" Asking for advice is better than making demands. It is like a dog wagging its tail and asking to be petted instead of growling and demanding to be petted.

Never threaten an employer or superior. "Unless I am paid more money, I am leaving" or "Unless I am promoted, I am going to look for another job" are statements that can mean certain death for one's continued employment. Whenever anyone made such a statement to me, I usually began looking for his or her replacement. No dog is dumb enough to demand more food by threatening, but some humans are.

Alerting people to possible danger or problems, as Sadie does when she barks at an approaching stranger or a passing aggressive dog, is another legitimate form of human barking that can save lives and inform people who can make critical decisions. I have owned several General Motors (GM) cars during my lifetime but fortunately did not own one between 2005 and 2015. During that time, GM built and sold millions of cars with a defective ignition switch that caused cars to unexpectedly shut down. Reportedly, more than one hundred people died in accidents caused by this defect, and many more were injured.[3] GM engineers knew about the problem as early as 2005 but did not disclose the issue. Subsequently GM recalled almost thirty million cars and made repairs. The company was fined by the National Transportation Safety Board and set up a fund to compensate victims.

I had a few meetings with GM officials regarding real estate deals years ago. They always sent lots of people to meetings. At one meeting, I was with one colleague from the Detroit office and probably twenty GM officials. When I asked my colleague who the decision maker was from GM, he told me the guy couldn't come to that meeting. My impression was that GM operated an inclusive culture with lots of layers of people involved in decision-making. It is inconceivable to me that only a few people might have known about the ignition problem at GM. If someone who knew the situation at GM had "barked" earlier, many deaths and injuries would likely have been avoided.

Patti owned a Toyota previously and was in an accident that extensively damaged her car. Fortunately, the airbags did not deploy. Takata Corporation, a Japanese company, had installed faulty airbags in more than one hundred million cars worldwide between 2002 and 2008, including Toyotas. When deployed, the bags sometimes exploded with such force that passengers were killed or injured. The company was forced to recall and repair the faulty airbags under government orders following a *New York Times* report accusing the company of knowing about the faulty airbags but not disclosing this information to governmental officials. A "barking" employee may have prevented these deaths and injuries. Now Patti owns a different car with another brand of airbag. She was fortunate.

If an employee sees something that is inappropriate or unethical, it is his or her responsibility to raise the issue with executives. No one should work or live in an unethical environment. No dog should remain silent when barking is the right thing to do, and no job is worth losing one's self-respect by countenancing wrong behavior. The consequences of doing nothing are generally worse than the consequences of speaking up.

Philosopher John Stuart Mill, in his classic essay, *On Liberty*, agrees: "A person may cause evil to others not only by his actions but by his inaction, and in either case is justly accountable to them for injury."[4]

## Alerting people to problems is a legitimate form of human barking.

For years, pollution levels in Beijing were excessive and hazardous to the health of citizens and visitors. One of my staff once attended a conference in Beijing. The conference included a field trip to a nearby city in China that was designed to be free of pollution. Unfortunately, the pollution in Beijing that day was so bad that the bus driver could not see, and the trip had to be canceled. The Chinese government refused to acknowledge a pollution problem in Beijing. In 2008, the US embassy in Beijing installed an air quality monitor on the rooftop and began tweeting hourly air quality readings. The Chinese government denounced the tweets and pressured the United States to cease its monitoring and announcements; the US embassy persisted. Eventually, in 2013, under pressure from its citizens, the Chinese government installed air quality monitors in the city and began a program to reduce the dangerous levels of pollution. The US embassy's "barking" amid threats successfully warned everyone, and changes were eventually instituted.

Bear, a six-year-old shepherd mix, barks at almost everything. Any outside noise triggers barking, even though it is usually just someone walking by. If a dog is walking by, Bear's barking intensifies. If he hears a noise that resembles a knock, or if someone actually comes to the front door, Bear's barking becomes frantic. Bear barks too much. Wade, Bear's owner, believes Bear is neurotic, and his neurosis reminds Wade of a former boss who was obsessive about micromanaging every decision and approving every action, no matter how minor. Such managers would cause less employee stress and encourage improved productivity if they barked less.

When I was CEO of Center America Property Trust, we were sued because a customer at a nearby shopping center claimed to have suffered emotional damage when the bank he was visiting was robbed. When we explained that we did not own the bank or the shopping center, the litigant proposed we pay a reduced amount anyway to settle the case. This kind of barking is irritating.

Too much barking can also cause people to ignore the frequent barking because they tire of responding. Aesop's fable "The Boy Who Cried Wolf," which probably dates to around 600 BC, describes the risk of raising false alarms.[5] This still applies to people and dogs in the twenty-first century.

Organizational policies should encourage moral and ethical behavior and should encourage employees to spotlight behaviors that are contrary to such policies. Opportunities to report transgressions or raise questions anonymously are standard with better-run organizations.

## No one should work or live in an unethical environment.

For years, sexual harassment was tolerated in many companies and organizations. Victims often did not register complaints because they feared losing their jobs or status, and when complaints were filed, they were often ignored. In more recent times, victims are "barking" complaints about bad and unacceptable behavior, and the chorus of barking has led to resignations of senior executives and widespread changes in practice and policy. Collective barking can be very effective by making too much noise for anyone to ignore.

The importance of moral and ethical behavior in business has become imbedded in better business schools. The prestigious Kelly School of Business at Indiana University, for example, has ten professors in its business ethics group, including Tim Fort, the chair in Business Ethics, whom I met and who owns and loves dogs. We discussed the business ethics of honesty and trust as well as dogs, which behave consistently with love, affection, and trust. Fort has published several books, including *Ethics and Governance*.[6] The Kelly School's focus on ethics in business is admirable and commendable.

In business and in life generally, don't be distracted; focus on what is really happening and what you can do about it. Don't hesitate to bark when the situation calls for it.

### Chapter Takeaways

1. Always act ethically and responsibly.
2. Alerting others to improper behavior is important.
3. Too much complaining and criticizing can be counterproductive.

Tug-of-war with Beau. © Peter Steusloff. Used with permission.

# 8

# Watching out for Hoses

© Martin Bucella. Used with permission.

**The other day I rolled in a big pile of bird poop;** *it must have been a really big bird. I thought I smelled pretty good, but Scott did not agree. He tried to give me a bath after the walk, but I don't care for baths. As soon as he picked up the hose, I pulled back and managed to slip out of my collar. I have mastered a certain technique to slip out of my collar, which I use in case of emergency—such as when Scott wants to give me a bath. Eventually, Scott succeeded in washing me, but it cost him an entire bag of dog treats, and he was soaked too by the time we were finished.*

*Many dog owners think giving a bath is spraying their dog with cold water from a hose. People would not do this to themselves. By contrast, humans step into a nice, warm, enclosed shower or ease themselves into a heated bathtub.*

*I know because I see this every day. If people were sprayed outside with cold water (including their private parts), I suspect they would not like taking baths or showers either. I hate it when someone says, "You smell like a dog." I am a dog. I don't need a "shower."*

*Dogs know it is important to avoid hoses. I know where the hoses are around my house and do not go near them. When Scott picks up a hose, I try to disappear. I also know to look for warning signs, like when he has the shampoo or a certain towel; then it is time to hide.*

*Hoses can come in various disguises, and I am always alert. Rosie has a dog-washing service van come to her house, for example. Rosie is like me—you will never get her to go to a dog wash store.*

*The other day I went over and checked the van out. The wash lady enticed Rosie into the van with treats and nice talk. Then she turned on the hose. If that van ever comes to my house, the woman won't trick me into going inside. She won't even be able to find me.*

*Not all hoses are readily visible, even the ones at home. Some may be in the garage or inside a shed. It is important to be on the lookout not only for visible hoses but also for hoses that are not as apparent.*

\* \* \*

Like hoses to a dog, there are lots of pitfalls and setbacks that can be avoided in life and in management with proper planning and anticipation. Sometimes it is a challenge to plan and manage the expected; a greater challenge is to avoid or mitigate what can go wrong. A common saying is "Expect the unexpected." Others have offered similar advice; according to Heraclitus, a Greek philosopher who lived about 2,500 years ago, "if you do not expect the unexpected, you will not find it."[1]

We all have expectations based on previous experience. If our parents were married for fifty years, we assume we will be married forever. But often our history and experience cause us to take things for granted and miss the signs of change and unforeseen "hoses." When my ex-wife filed for divorce after thirty years of marriage, it was unexpected—a hose I did not see. Subsequently, I met many others who had the same experience. We were not looking for the unexpected and were oblivious to the causes.

When my brother and then my sister died, I was shocked. I knew people died—everyone dies—but not people close to me. I suspect there were lifestyle changes and preventive medical treatments that could have postponed their deaths. But none of us was expecting or anticipating the unexpected.

In January 2017, two dogs named Panda and Lucy were found huddled on train tracks in western Ukraine.[2] It was bitter cold, and the dogs had been missing for two to three days. Evidently one dog was injured by a passing train and could not move. I live near a train track, and I know that trains are surprisingly hard to hear when they are coming directly at you. The second dog stayed with the injured mate, providing warmth and comfort. Whenever a train came, the dogs ducked down and let the train pass overhead. When rescuers arrived, it took a while to convince the uninjured dog to let them approach her crippled friend, but eventually both were saved and returned to their owners. When someone encounters a major unexpected setback, he or she may require help. You can watch for hoses, but you can't always avoid them, and like Panda and Lucy, you may need help to recover.

A couple of months ago, I started to back my car out of a parking space at the neighborhood shopping center. I noticed someone else coming toward me, so I stopped. Unfortunately, he was not looking and ran into my car. He had been to that center hundreds of times and didn't notice a car partially backed out. Maybe he was distracted and assumed the lane was clear. The fact that something happened previously does not mean the same result will occur in the future. We always need to be alert, especially when we are in familiar places.

Avoiding hoses can be even more difficult if the hoses have since disappeared but their effect lingers. My neighbor and friend Pam Laidlaw is a psychologist and tells me that when someone is behaving badly—she calls it "entrenched unproductive behavior"—it may be due to things that happened long ago. Without understanding what happened and how it has affected the present, people can suffer the spray of an invisible hose without even realizing what is happening. If one is constantly feeling "hosed," one should probably ask for professional help in assessing whether the hose that sprayed them long ago has left lasting effects.

In personal relationships, avoiding unnecessary conflict may be comparable to Sadie's quest to avoid hoses. Social-personality psychologist Amie Gordon, PhD, draws on psychological research to suggest ways to minimize conflict when a partner does something that is not desired by the other partner and could trigger a major argument:

1. Refrain from making a snap judgment. First impressions are often right, but not always.
2. Look for dis-confirming (as opposed to confirming) information. Too often people seek information that supports their preconceived view.
3. Put yourself in your partner's shoes. Viewing what happened from his or her perspective can lead to greater understanding.
4. Don't try to figure out who is right. Sometimes neither side is completely right or wrong.
5. Ask your partner what he or she is thinking. Sometimes we focus only on articulating our viewpoint.[3]

Reducing conflict in a relationship is not the same as avoiding conflict by not acknowledging or discussing problems. Every relationship has issues and problems because people are different. Avoiding issues and conflicts usually causes them to build up until they become bigger and more difficult to resolve.

Many situations in life come with hoses. If every cloud has a silver lining, it is likely that every silver lining comes with a cloud. Some hoses are obvious, but others are not so apparent. Unless we are constantly on alert for hoses and potential problems, we may not notice them in time to avoid adverse consequences.

At times, hoses can be distracting when focus is needed. Occasionally, racehorses are given blinders to focus their vision on the track ahead and eliminate off-track distractions. Unlike horse racing, in a person's life, using blinders or intentionally ignoring a problem is not a good solution to recognizing or solving important issues. Pretending a problem does not exist does not make that problem disappear.

Some hoses are more like open fire hydrants and virtually impossible not to notice—yet many people remain oblivious. People who buy homes in flood plains, for example, know there is the possibility of being flooded, but they seem surprised when the floods arrive. They usually decline the opportunity to purchase inexpensive flood insurance despite the obvious risk of flooding.

People who live in earthquake zones, like me, know they live in active geologic areas, but many make no preparation. California has more than two thousand known earthquake faults. According to the Uniform California Earthquake Rupture Forecast, there is a 99.7 percent chance of a major earthquake of 6.7 or higher within the next thirty years.[4] Despite this near certainty of a major quake, only 10 percent of California homeowners carry earthquake insurance. Evidently, because an earthquake did not happen last week, they assume it will not happen next week.

The earth is becoming warmer, ice caps are melting, and ocean water levels are rising. This is factual.[5] But policy initiatives to reduce the pace of global warming continue to meet resistance, especially from politicians who find it convenient to deny scientific findings.

In business, changing market conditions and changing competition are clearly identifiable hoses (or threats). However, some hoses are less visible or predictable. Because we cannot see them, we need to remain flexible so that we can respond when they do appear. Flexibility includes contingency planning.

Everyone typically defines some course of action and proceeds based on an anticipated outcome—let's call it Plan A. It is what people expect based mostly on past experience and, to a lesser extent, intelligence. Reliance on experience, however, can result in undesired outcomes, and it is almost always important to have contingency plans for when Plan A does not work as expected.

When leasing a shopping center with a large vacancy a few years ago, agents may have automatically called Circuit City, Linens 'n Things, or Borders; these previously reliable space users are all gone and out of business. What was Plan B?

In management, we become accustomed to what has happened previously. Too often we are not focused on Plan B, or C, or D. When the unexpected happens, are we prepared? Do we look for the hoses in life to avoid the cold spray?

One time I asked the executives of a big bank why they approved a large loan request my company had made. The banker replied, "Every potential borrower comes in here with a plan, but sometimes the plan does not work out. You and your colleagues always come in with a plan, but then you tell us what the contingency plans are if the intended plan does not work. You and your team get credit for being realistic and planning for contingencies."

Sometimes the hoses are clearly visible but ignored. Many companies fail after years of poor competitive performance. Others fail because of excessive reliance on debt to fund operations. It is always surprising how executives, bankers, and employees act surprised when a company fails; such a result is almost always foreseeable. But most people are not looking for the hoses, and those who see the hoses often choose to ignore them.

Ed, a Labrador retriever who lives nearby, is always getting in trouble. Like all dogs, Ed likes to eat, especially human food. When his owner leaves food packages on the kitchen counter and leaves for a while, Ed can barely contain his excitement. He tries to remain calm until he hears the car leave the driveway, and then he stands on his hind legs to knock the food off the countertop. He eats the whole package as quickly as possible, fearing the return of the car and owner, but he leaves lots of crumbs and paper. He pretends to not know anything about the mess when confronted by his owner, but it is hard to be convincing when his face is still covered with crumbs. Admitting mistakes is always better than having someone else discover the problem.

Years ago, I was a regular customer of Blockbuster, the video rental store, which was founded in 1985 and soon became the dominant retailer offering movies and video games for rent. My companies made many deals with them to occupy space in our shopping centers. They were a highly desirable and popular tenant.

At its peak, Blockbuster had four thousand stores in the United States as well as a global presence. It moved into several related businesses in attempts to diversify, including Blockbuster music and online video rental. Blockbuster executives were very aware of the emergence of mail-in video rental and video streaming, but they failed to adjust to the shift in market preferences. In 2000, Blockbuster passed on the opportunity to buy Netflix for $50 million. In 2010 Blockbuster filed for bankruptcy. Netflix's recent valuation was about $33 billion. Blockbuster failed to respond to the hoses even when they were visible.

Badly managed organizations do not always fail; sometimes they just perform poorly. Often, organizations refuse to change as markets and conditions evolve and competition changes. They don't notice all the new hoses.

It is often not sufficient to solve an obvious or near-term problem. In business and in life, the focus is too often on only the next move. However, like good chess players, successful leaders often think multiple moves ahead.

There are many examples of companies that moved successfully forward, led the race for a few laps, and then fell behind as others outmaneuvered them. They identified the first hose but subsequently fell victim to other hoses they failed to see in time. They focused on the first move or short-term solution and not the required moves to sustain long-term success.

When I was growing up, for example, there were no mobile phones. We used landlines, and when we were not at home, we used pay telephones. The various Bell telephone companies were regulated monopolies. I recall a meeting with executives from the May Department Stores Company in the mid-1980s. One of the executives entered the meeting with a large, cumbersome portable telephone. It was the size of a small suitcase. He said it was the future, but we laughed at the thought of everyone lugging around a heavy piece of equipment. Like us that day, the dominant landline companies ignored the hoses of changing technology and continued focusing on their landlines while Motorola focused its attention on the new wireless phone technology.

Motorola successfully developed and marketed the first commercial mobile phones. They dominated the new industry. At one time, their flip phones were the most sought-after phones. However, they apparently did not think multiple moves ahead and did not migrate fast enough into smartphones with greater capabilities; they were subsequently surpassed by Apple, Google, Samsung, and others. Sometimes, we identify hoses in the past or present but forget to monitor for potential hoses in the future.

Like the television industry and the cable companies that emerged later, computer companies have experienced dramatic transitions in market position and leadership. Early in my career, I was responsible for detailed cash flow calculations for clients. Computers were not readily available, so my colleagues and I used calculators. Any change in a financial model required many calculations. Until personal computers were developed, financial modeling was a tedious and time-consuming job.

The early personal computer companies provided a wonderful product, but almost none survived the surge of competition. My favorite early computers were those made by Epson and Wang. Then IBM became the gold standard. None of these companies makes personal computers any longer. They went from using the hose to soak earlier technology users to suffering the spray from others that subsequently emerged, although IBM has repositioned itself as a technology service company.

It is impossible to avoid every hose every time, and mistakes are part of life. For example, several neighborhood shopping centers owned by Center

America were in lower-income neighborhoods where security and safety were customer and tenant concerns. In Houston, Center America made a few deals with the police department to put in-store front offices in at-risk-neighborhood shopping centers. However, in one such center, most of our existing tenants vacated the day the police station opened. Evidently, the tenants or their customers were conducting illegal activities in their otherwise normal business and needed to relocate when the police moved in. We did not expect that outcome when we negotiated the deal with the police department.

Sometimes, it's possible to identify the hose, make careful plans to avoid it, and yet still end up getting wet. At Investa, it was very clear that our home-building operation was losing considerable money and unlikely to return to profitability. We spun Clarendon Homes out of Investa into a separate stand-alone company with an independent board of directors and management team. The executive team thought the problem was solved until Clarendon's losses accelerated, and Investa had to reengage and cover the losses until we could sell the company years later.

Recently I was walking around the neighborhood with Sadie, and we encountered a black poodle that was running free and unleashed. Sadie barked loudly and confrontationally at him, perhaps chastising him for not being on a leash. The poodle quickly jumped on Sadie and pinned her down until I intervened. Even someone as perceptive as Sadie can misjudge and make mistakes.

Success is often the result of being aware of what could go wrong and making plans accordingly. We should always have a contingency plan ready, like knowing how to escape and which way to go if we misjudge another dog or person. We will still make mistakes but likely will make far fewer missteps if we watch out for those hoses.

## Chapter Takeaways

1. Be aware of what could go wrong.
2. **Even the best plans often do not work out as expected.**
3. **Expect the unexpected.**

# 9

# Embracing Change

© Martin Bucella. Used with permission.

*As a puppy, I lived with my mother in the wild. We had lots of fun chasing squirrels and rabbits, foraging for food, and playing. I did not want change, but then my mom and I got sick.*

*Even though my mother taught me to avoid human beings, we were still captured by the side of a busy highway. We were both hungry and sick.*

*Later, I moved to Austin and lived with Ross. He took care of me and nursed me back to health. He played with me when he was not in school or at work. And I hung out with Duke, Matt's dog. Matt was Ross's roommate. Life was good. I slept on Ross's bed when he was not there and played with Duke, who was not as quick or smart as I. I never wanted my new life to change.*

*But change happens. One day, Ross put me into a big crate, which was placed in the body of a big jet plane. I was alone and afraid. It was cold, and*

*I did not know where Ross was. A few hours later, the plane landed, and the crate was moved to a building. Then Ross rescued me again, and I met Ross's dad, Scott.*

*Initially I hated living in a new house with Scott; I missed Ross and Matt and Duke. But I have lived with Scott for a few years now, and life is good. I go to the beach almost every day, run off leash, hang out with other dogs, look for treats, and smell other dogs' pee. It is a lot of fun. I never expected or wanted change, but it all worked out.*

*Not every change is good; I have met dogs who moved into big houses when times were good and received lots of treats, pats, and walks. But when times change, the attention disappears. This is especially true when the owners have a child and then ignore the dog.*

*My advice to dogs that suffer such an event is to make friends with the new kid. I made friends with Scott's granddaughter, and little Claire actually throws food to me at mealtimes, especially when the adults are not looking.*

\* \* \*

Most humans do not appear to like change. Like dogs, humans are comforted by routine and familiarity and are uncomfortable with events that disrupt the security that is afforded by the familiar. Yet change is ever present. Every day we change, circumstances change, and our environment changes; but we may not notice the incremental nature of such changes. Heraclitus, the Greek philosopher who lived around 500 BC, advised (what has been loosely translated as), "There is nothing permanent except change."[1]

Within communities, there seems to be a constituency of the status quo. Some people always prefer what exists to the uncertainty of what could be. Whenever a new project is proposed, no matter how attractive or otherwise desirable, there seems to be resistance.

There are a number of residents in Del Mar, where I live, who seem to be uncomfortable with change. Del Mar's dated downtown commercial area still looks much like it did in the 1950s and 1960s. If people had prevented change then, it would still look like the 1930s. Just because something is old does not mean it is desirable. But some residents are more comfortable with what they know than with the unpredictability that comes with change.

I served on the local community design review board (DRB). Whenever someone proposes a new house or commercial building or even external changes to an existing building, it must be approved by the DRB. Rarely is a proposal submitted without some neighborhood opposition. Even when a beautiful new home is proposed to replace an older, obsolete, and poorly maintained house, some neighbors typically protest. They like the current view. They like the existing trees. They are comfortable with the status quo and are concerned the change will bring unknown and possibly undesired results.

My awareness of community resistance to change dates back to when I was a young man working as an intern at the National Capital Planning Commission in Washington, DC, in 1971. I spent the summer between my years at graduate school coordinating public hearings on the then-proposed Metro subway system. The alignment of the Orange line passed directly under Georgetown, which was congested at the time. The local residents turned out in great numbers to protest against any station in Georgetown, fearing undesirable people would come to Georgetown if the subway provided good access. Largely due to public opposition, a station was never built at Georgetown, and the congestion has continued to worsen while other metro stops, including in nearby northern Virginia, have generated considerable new investment, shopping, offices, and residences. Fear of the unknown caused Georgetown residents to fight against change, to the detriment of future generations.

I have worked on many new commercial real estate developments, and there is almost always neighborhood opposition, especially in more affluent communities. When shopping center projects are eventually approved and built, often the same people who were strident in opposition are at the grand opening, eager to take advantage of the new shopping opportunities. Residents typically fear the unknown but embrace the projects after they are built, and they come to realize that their earlier fears were unfounded.

We must deal with change in everyday life, but some changes cause more disruption than others, especially when families are affected. Moving to a new home and neighborhood can be exciting but can also trigger fear of the unknown. Changing schools can be particularly worrisome, although children often seem more adaptable than adults. I remember moving from the nearby beaches of San Diego to the humidity of Houston when Andrew was entering high school and Ross was in fourth grade. It was strange to walk through Andrew's new high school without knowing a single person there after being involved with his old school and friends. Fortunately, Houston turned out to be a nice place with good neighbors, and we all adjusted. Ross actually moved back to Houston after law school.

In my experience, changing jobs can be a great challenge and cause for considerable stress. I moved to new jobs many times. At work, my new colleagues and employees did not know me and were wary of me, especially when I arrived as the new boss. My accent was often different, my background may have been different, and my approach to problem solving and employee interaction likely represented a different path. Relating, understanding the environment, and connecting to what exists are all challenges to a newcomer. Changing what exists, including established practices, procedures, systems, and staffing, is an even greater challenge. But I always kept my perspective and experience in mind when confronting these challenges; a different perspective was likely what the company needed.

In addition to the stress at work, changing locations and jobs can trigger significant stress at home. Taking care of a family with every member experiencing his or her own stress and apprehension adds to the burden, but looking out for family is essential for a successful transition.

When my family and I moved to Houston from San Diego, I made sure I was home for dinner almost every night. We always talked about the boys' day before they went to sleep. They knew I was there for them, and this provided some relief for my wife. After the children went to sleep, I went into the study and resumed work when necessary, before going to bed later. Had I stayed at work until I was finished, I would not have been home for dinner and able to support my family when they needed it most. Embracing change often means making accommodations and adjustments.

Accepting the idea that one needs medical intervention for a condition not previously experienced or easily recognized is difficult and requires accepting an unwanted change. The most threatening conditions are the most difficult to accept. My sister, Judy, had a persistent cough but insisted it was just an irritant. A week later she died of a blood clot. In recent decades the medical profession has made significant progress in diagnosing medical maladies and addressing them, but individuals still need to recognize that changes to their health cannot be viewed through the familiar lens of past experience. I suffered a transient ischemic attack (TIA), a minor stroke, and had no idea what was happening to me. Fortunately, my colleagues called an ambulance. When confronted by an unfamiliar medical condition, everyone needs to act and seek medical care. Checking the internet for diagnosis and advice is not a substitute for seeing a doctor.

Personal relationships change and evolve over time and require constant recognition and adjustments. Within families, the personal relationship

Parker lived with two other dogs but was the smartest one. He was also constantly getting into the garbage and as a result was often in trouble. Then Sarah, his owner, bought a secure trash can—the kind with a pedal you have to step on to open. Parker soon learned how to open the trash can and pull out anything edible. After Parker finished eating anything good, he exited, and the other two dogs made a mess with the papers and trash. Sometimes they even knocked over the can. Whenever Sarah came home to the mess, she always blamed the other dogs until, years later, she saw Parker carefully push the pedal and pull stuff out of the can while the other dogs watched. When change came, Parker learned to adapt.

between spouses changes when the children grow up and move away. Personal dynamics change as partners age, when one or both retire and spend more time at home, and when financial needs are not as challenging, affording more freedom and choices. Adjusting to such significant changes is a major challenge to any long-term relationship.

Terri Orbuch, psychologist and author of *5 Simple Steps to Take Your Marriage from Good to Great*,[2] analyzed 373 couples over a period of about thirty years. Based on interviews and analysis, she recommends five steps to sustain a long-term relationship:

1. Expect less and get more from your partner. A key problem is frustration when a partner's expectations go unmet.
2. Give incentives and rewards. Don't take a partner for granted; let him or her know that he or she is special and valued.
3. Have daily briefings for improved communication. Don't limit discussion to "maintaining the household" topics.
4. Implement change. Avoid or mitigate relationship ruts by introducing new, mutual activities.
5. Keep costs low and benefits high. Happy couples typically have five positive experiences with their partner for every one negative encounter.[3]

All relationships have negative and positive elements. Successful couples, according to Orbuch, focus on the positives.

As we move through life, we become accustomed to the routine. We are used to doing things a certain way that has provided comfort and satisfaction in the past. However, at least for humans, the familiar path may not lead to a better place. The best way forward usually involves accepting and embracing change. We need to constantly look for new ways to do things if we are to improve our circumstances.

Transportation planners often deal with drivers accustomed to the familiar path. Planners sometimes categorize car drivers as "sheep" and "goats." Most people drive to work the same way every day. Even when new transportation improvements provide a more efficient way to work, most (the sheep) continue their old route to work without change. A few, more venturesome drivers (the goats), however, are always searching for a better way. They quickly find the better, newer path and become leaders. Eventually the sheep follow them to the new route and faster journey.

In business, resistance to change follows a similar course to that of life generally. Executives take comfort in doing what has worked previously. As discussed in previous chapters, adjusting to changing conditions is often essential for organizational survival.

---

## It is most important to initiate change before an organization feels the need to change.

---

However, moving in new directions and with unprecedented products requires risk and uncertainty. Two industries, commercial book publishing and filmmaking, have become risk averse due to changing economics in their business.

Book publishing is typically not very profitable, and resistance to change and innovation is driven by concerns about lack of financial success—especially with books written by new or unknown authors. There are exceptions, but about 99 percent of books published never make sufficient revenue to recover costs.[4] As a result, commercial publishers generally insist on following tested, familiar formats such as publishing well-known authors. When I asked one publisher what I could do to gain their interest in publishing my first book, her reply was to change my name to Bill Clinton.

Similarly, movie studios prefer sequels over innovative new movies because of perceived lower risk. If a movie was popular and successful, there is a greater likelihood that a sequel will build on the original success. Seventeen of the top twenty grossing films of all time are sequels.[5] Studios are reluctant to risk failure of an untested concept without clear precedents. Resistance to change and innovation is sometimes based on industry economics and the greater probability of achieving financial success by staying with previously successful formats.

Although some organizations resist change due to demonstrated economic considerations, some resist change even though current and past methods are clearly unsuccessful. This is often true when political considerations are involved. The US government placed an embargo on shipments to Cuba in 1960. Supporters predicted the Cuban government would fall as a result. More than fifty years later, the embargo remains in place, as does the government of Cuba. An expression for staying the course despite its obvious failure has been attributed to Albert Einstein: "Insanity is doing the same thing over and over again and expecting different results."[6]

Many leaders in history have encouraged others to embrace change. For example, former president John F. Kennedy said, "Change is the law of life. Those who look only to the past or present are certain to miss the future."[7]

There are many examples of companies and organizations that have embraced change and profited as a result. Once I was negotiating a deal with representatives of the Walt Disney Company, for example, and was given a behind-the-scenes tour of Disney's famous animation department. Disney achieved its dominant market position in film as a result of its animators, who produced such iconic characters as Mickey Mouse and Donald Duck and such classic films as *Cinderella* and *Snow White*. When digital animation eventually replaced hand-drawn figures, Disney bought Pixar, the leading digital filmmaker with such hits as *Toy Story*. Subsequently, Disney bought Lucasfilm and acquired the leading high-tech digital effects studio, Industrial Light & Magic, along with the *Star Wars* franchise. As a result of change and repositioning as markets evolved, Disney has retained its dominant market position.

Disney has also profited by extending its brand to theme parks, retail stores, retail goods and merchandise, and a variety of branded products. As it creates brand characters in its films, it merchandises the new brands in a variety of formats. Disney is a company that has been able to reinvent itself continually.

By contrast, there are many companies that were once market leaders but lost leadership and profitability due to their failure to embrace change as quickly as markets evolved. Eastman Kodak was founded in 1888 and dominated the global market for camera and photographic film for most of the twentieth century. Like almost everyone in my generation, I bought Kodak film, took pictures with a film camera, and sent the film to a developer—often Kodak—for prints, which were usually provided on Kodak paper.

Kodak is credited with inventing the key technology for digital cameras, but the company was slow to adjust to the emerging market for digital photography. Its executives apparently feared loss of profits from the photographic film if digital cameras became widely accepted and thought that if they chose not to emphasize the digital format, it would delay or stop the migration to digital photography. Instead, other companies like Nikon, Canon, and Sony became the dominant camera companies, and Kodak was forced to file for bankruptcy in 2012.

Oddly, it is most important to initiate change before an organization feels the need to change. When an organization is performing well and making good profits or providing excellent services, it is usually easier to raise funds for new initiatives, attract new employees or volunteers, and gain acceptance of new ideas. When conditions are already declining and markets are moving away from an organization's core expertise, that organization often must focus on survival, including through reduction of costs. Frequently, new competitors become established and threaten to displace the previous market leaders.

Unfortunately, it is more typical for organizations to resist change when times are good and miss the opportunity to continue their success into the future. Jack Welch, former CEO of General Electric, advises companies, "Change before you have to."[8]

---

## With change comes risk, and not all change results in success.

---

F. W. Woolworths dominated general merchandise retailing in the early to mid-1900s. Almost every town had a Woolworths. There was a Woolworths store where I grew up in Berwyn, Illinois. It opened with great fanfare at Cermak Plaza in 1956.

Woolworths opened its first store in 1878 and grew to become one of the largest retail chains in the world, but the company's stores declined when customers moved to the suburbs and Kmart and Walmart arrived with new formats, locations, and merchandising systems. Despite having the early mover market advantage, Woolworths closed in 1997 because it failed to change, leaving the opportunity to serve America's retail customers to what was previously a little-known store from Arkansas named Walmart.

In business, failure to change almost always leads to poor performance. Markets change, competitors evolve, and new products and services are developed. The history of business is littered with failed enterprises that were not sufficiently innovative and did not evolve as their markets changed, like Kodak, Polaroid, Woolworths, Pan Am, Blockbuster, and so on. As discussed earlier, watching out for "hoses" associated with change is an ongoing process, and onetime adjustments and innovations often do not survive subsequent events and product evolution.

With change comes risk, and not all change results in favorable outcomes. Success requires trying new approaches or creating new products or services. One of my favorite sayings is "You have to kiss a lot of frogs before you find a prince."

There are ways to embrace change but also identify and reduce risks involved. When Sadie meets a new dog, both dogs typically smell each other before deciding how to proceed. People don't sniff each other, but we can take time to analyze what is changing, why, and the possible consequences as the change continues.

### Chapter Takeaways

1. Change is inevitable. Accept and adjust.
2. Be flexible and mobile to accommodate change.
3. Be sensitive to how change affects others.

Sadie on her favorite couch watching for the UPS driver.

# 10

# Being a Good Sniffer

© Martin Bucella. Used with permission.

*I sniff a lot.* I sniff bushes, grass, dirt, and even streets. Sometimes, I put my nose in the air and just sniff the air. Scott thinks I sniff too much, but it is important to know where I am and what's happening around me. Once I had to find my way home without a human, and I was able to retrace my path for over a mile crossing streets and trails. Good thing I sniffed on my way there.

When I lived with my mother in the wild, we found food by sniffing. If we had been unable to sniff, we would not have survived.

I find lots of good sniffs now by watching other dogs like Buddy and Rosie. They are good sniffers too. Whenever they linger at a spot, I trot over to sniff what they found. It's usually pretty good and something I would not have discovered by myself. Once Buddy found a whole box of bagels, so I happily had a bagel for my breakfast.

*The other morning, I found two pieces of pizza in the bushes next to the beach. I grabbed one piece and ran onto the beach with it so Scott could not catch me and take it away. Scott is not very fast, and I can actually eat while I run. After I finished my pizza, we walked up the long beach and back. All I could think about on the walk was the second piece of pizza still in the bushes. Finally, as we approached the end of the walk, I hurried ahead, grabbed the second piece, ran off with it so neither humans nor dogs could steal it, and gobbled it down. Good sniffing that day paid off twice.*

*In addition to searching for food, I look for the scent of other dogs, prey, and potentially dangerous animals like coyotes. I can tell if another dog, animal, or person has been in the area and if I need to be on alert.*

\* \* \*

People don't sniff very well, but we can use our other senses to "sniff" and understand the environments in which we live and work. Sniffing is a way of identifying what is changing as well as understanding the circumstances and environment in which we live and work. Many people go about their day, whether at work, at school, or at home, focused only on their routine and responsibilities. They often become complacent and do not take the time or put forth sufficient effort to study, or sniff, the surrounding environment. Understanding one's surroundings and how they are changing is important for life and work.

Acquiring useful information is how humans sniff. One can never know too much. Reading is probably the most critical means of learning. About 2,500 years ago, the Chinese philosopher Confucius is said to have advised, "You cannot open a book without learning something."[1] Today, with the advent of the internet and the digital revolution, there is considerable information available to anyone who wants to expand his or her knowledge. One can find most information on the internet, but television news, National Public Radio, newspapers, and magazines like the *Economist* are filled with useful information documenting the world in which we all live.

Unfortunately, many people use their free time to seek entertainment instead of information. They are not sniffing. Perhaps everyone should follow Dr. Seuss's advice: "The more you read, the more things you know. The more you learn, the more places you'll go."[2]

Sniffing and knowing one's surroundings is important in one's personal life. Relationships evolve over time; not sniffing every day may mean that one misses the changes underway and thus misses the opportunity to stay

Nanuk, a mixed-breed rescue dog from Texas, liked to hang out with the Mexican construction workers in his neighborhood. Initially they were not interested in engaging with Nanuk, but he persisted when he sniffed the food in their lunch boxes; in time, he became a favorite visitor. He knew exactly when the workers took a lunch break every day, and subsequently, they often shared their tacos with him. Once Scott was looking for Nanuk, and the workers all shouted Nanuk's name in heavily accented English to let him know Scott was looking for him. Nanuk became good friends with these immigrant workers. Nice people often share what they have even if their possessions are modest. It doesn't matter what they look like or where they came from or even what language they speak.

connected. How many times have we met couples who say "We just grew apart"? No one was sniffing, I suspect.

Long-term relationships appear to require more sniffing and communication, which seems counterintuitive but is consistent with changes that naturally occur in such relationships. Divorces among older Americans have doubled in the past decade, and about 25 percent of all divorces include someone at least fifty years of age. Perhaps we become too accustomed to the routine and are not seeing the changes that happen right in front of us.

Sniffing leads to understanding the context in which we live and how we relate to others. Knowing that someone's husband has cancer is critical to understanding why that person is acting in a particular way. Knowing that someone has a key exam or deadline the next day may explain why he or she is not focused on what someone else is saying. Acquiring information that is important and affects those around us leads to better understanding and personal connections.

In business, there are multiple environments that are important to recognize and monitor. The market environment for one's products is critical. Where is demand coming from? What is the likely future of those demand sources? Is it necessary to find new sources of demand to offset future weaknesses?

When working for a company or organization, one should always be aware of market changes that could affect the future viability of one's employer. In the early 1980s, when I ran a consulting division in Evanston, Illinois, a major source of my business was shopping center developers seeking market studies and tenant sales forecasts. A friend of mine was hired by a developer to provide the same services in-house. Then another friend was hired by another developer for the same reason. A trend in the industry became clear: the nation's big real estate developers were bringing work in-house that had been previously outsourced to consultants. I realized our business, which relied on developers outsourcing financial and market forecasts, would struggle. When I was contacted by the Hahn Company, a major development company in California, and offered an attractive job to undertake work that consultants had been doing, I accepted. If someone knows a business will not succeed over time, he or she should not hang around and wait for someone else to turn the lights off.

Sniffing is understanding the environment and anticipating what may happen next. Sniffing is not change in itself; rather, it helps anticipate changes that are coming.

Service organizations operate in an ever-changing environment and often must cope with changing customer needs, demographic shifts, and changes in funding sources and requirements. Failure to anticipate these changes and redirect efforts may lead to organizational underperformance or even failure.

Publicly supported organizations often need to change as funding availability changes. In recent years, public universities have been confronted with significant requirements for change due to diminished funds for education. Activities and processes born in a time of greater funding availability are changing, such as using less expensive, nontenured faculty to teach classes; incorporating digitally available lectures and lesson plans; and continuing to provide tenure for professors whose expertise is in high demand.

The medical profession is renowned for sniffing—looking for changes and studies that can lead to improved health care. At hospitals, sniffing and testing new procedures, medications, and instruments can improve care and save lives. Hospitals are frequently surveyed and compared to understand best practices and outcomes. Changes are often made slowly, however, because lives are affected. Similarly, pharmaceutical companies are constantly testing new drugs to mitigate or cure medical maladies.

Competition changes often, and it is critical to know what competitors are doing. When I worked in the homebuilding business, I spent most of the time monitoring what other builders were selling, not unlike Sadie watching what other dogs are sniffing. Homebuilders needed to move quickly to respond to any successful new products, or they would lose the opportunity.

Unfortunately, the homebuilding company I worked for was owned by a large conglomerate and was unable to act quickly when speed was required. Because of required layers of approval and associated budgetary delays, we were often much slower than our smaller, more nimble competitors to bring new houses with desirable features to market. Despite a good market and profitable competitors, the company I worked for subsequently failed.

## Sniffing has become big business.

Some retailers are often good at sniffing new fashion trends and moving quickly to respond to consumer demand. Many of the shopping centers I worked on, especially in Europe, had a Zara store as an anchor tenant. Zara is a fashion retailer with a headquarters in La Coruna, a town located in the remote northwest corner of Spain. Zara and its retail owner, Inditex, are one of the world's largest and most successful retailers, with annual sales over $20 billion.

Zara's typical customers are young adults with an appetite for inexpensive fashion. Their fashion desires change quickly and frequently, making it a challenge for retailers that typically have long order lead times, lengthy designer and production timetables, and distinct fashion seasons. Zara has contributed to revolutionary changes in retail logistics by expediting the process of identifying fashion trends, designing new clothes to respond to the trends, producing the clothes, and supplying the stores with the updated fashions very quickly.

Zara typically delivers fashion merchandise to stores around the world twice a week. The company can usually replenish a hot-selling item in two weeks. It can produce a new fashion item to respond to an opportunity quickly because it controls and coordinates design, planning, merchandising, and production functions. The company owns many highly automated factories in Spain, so it does not have to outsource production to Asia, and through agreements, it controls hundreds of finishing shops in Spain and Portugal, which further expedites the design-to-store logistics.

Zara is not the only retailer that can identify a fashion trend, design merchandise to respond to the new trend, produce the merchandise in a highly cost-efficient process, and deliver the merchandise to retail stores in a short time frame. But Zara's successful track record of growth and profitability demonstrates its exceptional sniffing ability coupled with delivery capability.

Sniffing or using statistical analytics has become critical in sports, including baseball. I have always been a baseball fan; as a youngster, I followed the Chicago Cubs, and now I have season tickets to the San Diego Padres. Sniffing using data and detailed analyses has become the norm in baseball. The trend was documented in the 2003 book *Moneyball*, which described the use of statistical analyses to evaluate and rank a player's worth to a team (the Oakland Athletics).[3] Subsequently, virtually all major-league baseball teams began using data and statistics to assist in making baseball decisions on players and on field strategy. I wish the Cubs had used data when I was younger, and I hope the Padres can successfully use analytical tools to become more competitive.

Today, baseball pitchers typically review the hitting tendencies of each player on the opposing team before each game. They review scouting reports on each opposing player, look at spray charts that pinpoint where a player has hit every single ball over the course of a year, and review detailed notes on how a player responds to specific ball and strike counts and types of pitches. A *Wall Street Journal* article on the former Dodgers and current Diamondbacks pitcher, Zack Greinke, says in reference to Greinke, "He'll find out in a 2–2 count, the guy is 0 for 20 on outside pitches but 10 for 20 on sliders."[4] Greinke and other successful pitchers know which pitch is most likely to be successful in light of a batter's statistical tendencies, pitch count, outs, base runners, and field alignment.

Hitters similarly study tendencies of opposing pitchers, including which pitches are typically thrown in different situations. Managers analyze opposing hitter spray charts to position the fielders for each hitter, according to the hitter's statistical tendencies. There is an increasing tendency to shift infielders to one side of the infield when a particular batter consistently hits to one side. Sometimes, fielders are shifted only when the count of balls and strikes reaches a level that increases a particular batter's tendency to hit in a specific area.

Often pitchers and hitters view video clips of the opposing players' performance under different circumstances. Baseball has become a game of big data manipulation to increase the probability of success. It is not too different in intent from Sadie's more primitive sniffing, however.

Sniffing has become big business for technology giants like Google and Facebook. Using big data and mathematical algorithms, Google, Facebook, and others identify consumption preferences and target product advertising to likely consumers. Like more than a billion other people, I have a Google account. The other day I was curious about what Google knew about me, so I looked at my Google profile. I was amazed; it tracked and recorded every website I visited and every inquiry I made. It knows what music I like, what sports I follow, and where I obtain my news. It knows what products I am investigating or buying and what trips I am considering. I assume it sells this information to marketing departments. Google, Facebook, and others have revolutionized the advertising industry and customer marketing generally.

One always needs to be alert to changes in relationships, business, and life generally. Unless one is always sniffing, one may miss what is different and be unable to adjust in a timely manner to survive and prosper.

### Chapter Takeaways

1. **Always be alert to the surrounding environment.**
2. **Try to detect changes that are occurring in personal relationships and at work.**
3. **Never become too content or too comfortable with the present.**

# 11

# Chasing Cars

© Martin Bucella. Used with permission.

**Dogs like to chase things.** *It is especially fun to chase squirrels and rabbits but almost impossible to catch either. There is a rabbit that lives in Scott's neighbor Vicki's yard. Whenever I see him, I give chase. He is a clever rabbit, and I have not caught him yet. One day I will catch him, but he is fast and sneaky. With squirrels, at least I have the satisfaction of making them climb and stay in trees.*

*My friend Cooper likes to chase birds on the beach. Sometimes the birds are even bigger than Cooper. He never comes close to catching a bird but feels good and proud about making them fly away after chasing them. Another friend, Nola, a black-and-brown German shepherd mixed with maybe a greyhound—she is really fast—chases birds too. Between Nola and Cooper, the sea birds spend a lot of time flying.*

*I like to chase other dogs and be chased, especially by dogs that are slower than me. The other day I was running with Rosie and Beau, who are both fast. They had me squeezed with one on either side, and I could not outrun them. So, I slowed down suddenly, and their momentum carried them past me. I turned and ran the other way before they figured out what happened.*

*Chasing bicyclists and runners gets me in trouble. Humans who run or bike freak out when a dog shows sign of chasing.*

*I used to chase joggers on the beach if I thought they wanted to play. Once it was pretty cold, and a woman runner was wearing big mittens on her hands. The mittens looked just like some of my toys, so I jumped as she passed by, grabbed a mitten, and played keep-away from Scott—and everyone else on the beach. It was lots of fun for a while, but Scott got mad at me. I had to go to dog training with someone named Hector after that.*

*Another time there was a guy running in a pair of bright-red shorts. I could not resist jumping and pulling at the shorts as he ran by. Unfortunately, the shorts ripped, and he was mad even after Scott offered to pay for the shorts. I think that is when Scott decided to buy my shock collar.*

*Fortunately, I didn't need to wear the shock collar very long, because I quickly realized if I refrained from chasing joggers, I would not be shocked. Before Scott pressed the shock button, he played music on the collar. I hated that music. Soon I stopped chasing joggers completely. After a week, Scott took off the collar, and now I don't even look at joggers unless I smell treats as they pass by.*

*Chasing cats that run and climb trees is fun. But some cats don't run when confronted by a dog. They hiss and show their claws. There is a cat like this who lives just around the corner, and I try to avoid even looking at him. I do not like cats.*

*Chasing cars can be fun, even if I don't catch them. I like chasing buses and noisy trucks even more. Usually I just lunge at the vehicles as they pass and don't try to catch them.*

\* \* \*

Dogs may be natural chasers, but so are humans. We chase success, we chase good jobs and careers, we chase prospective partners and spouses, and we chase what we value and want to catch. Our pursuits are not that different from those of dogs, just more complicated. And, like dogs, we need to be prepared for what to do if our chase is successful.

Probably the most important chase in someone's life is finding and securing the right partner or spouse. With regard to catching a spouse or partner, the *New York Times* had a column a few years ago suggesting the world was full of people whose desirability as a partner could be rated on a scale of one to ten, with ten being the most desirable mate. As I recall, the columnist characterized humanity as sixes chasing sevens and being pursued by fives. As long as the sixes realize they are not going to catch a ten, there is no reason not to aim for a seven, but they should be prepared to accept a six or five. A favorite phrase of mine, "Pursuit of perfection is at the expense of the very good," is often repeated and has many sources and variations.[1] It seems especially applicable for identifying partners and future spouses.

Billy Joe, a man who grew up in Appalachia and worked on the factory assembly line with me many years ago, did not believe in chasing tens or even fives. "Scott," he said, "you will be better off if you marry an ugly woman; she'll appreciate you a lot more." I did not take Billy Joe's advice, but Billy Joe was always a happy guy.

My advice with regard to partners in life is to find someone who is loving and kind. A nice person will be more supportive and understanding than someone whose primary attractions are beauty, money, achievement, or fame. I agree with Shakespeare: "Kindness in women, not their beauteous looks, shall win my love."[2]

People always must be careful what they chase because they may catch it. If one wants the benefits of a married life or partnership, one should be prepared to give up a more self-focused single life in which decisions are one's own. Deciding to marry and give up single life is a major milestone, and thereafter life is a compromise. Having a child is the greatest event in life, but life afterward is much and forever changed.

Buying a house and assuming a big mortgage represents another successful chase. However, it constrains life choices, such as going from two incomes to one at a later date or taking overseas vacations. Yet it also provides a supportive and shared home environment, especially for a family that will be there long after the vacation has passed. It is usually a good investment too.

However, buying a house that is too expensive and for which the future mortgage payments are unaffordable is not a good catch. Such actions led to the global financial crisis of 2009 and bankrupted many.

Gaining acceptance to a preferred and select university is a major achievement. However, the cost of attending is likely to be high and, unless there are financial aid grants available, attending the school could result in

 Sometimes catching something that is highly desired involves creativity, flexibility, and even a clever sense of definition. There is a story about a salesman who wanted a dog and was driving through a rural area. A sign outside a rundown house proclaimed, "Dog for sale." The salesman knocked on the door and was introduced to a friendly mixed-breed dog.

"How much do you want for the dog?" he inquired.

The owner said, "One million dollars and not a penny less."

The salesman departed quickly. A couple years later, the salesman was passing by the same house and decided to stop and ask about the dog.

"I sold it," said the owner.

"How much did you get?" asked the salesman.

"One million dollars," replied the owner.

"Someone gave you one million dollars in cash for that dog?" asked the salesman incredulously.

"No," replied the owner. "I traded him for two five-hundred-thousand-dollar cats."

---

excessive levels of student debt. The decision to attend any particular college should be coupled with an understanding of costs and available financial aid for most students and their families.

The chase is a natural instinct for dogs and humans. We are born to chase. But chasing unattainable goals makes no sense and is a waste of time. The odds of winning the Powerball lottery were about 175 million to 1, but this was changed in 2015 to make the odds worse and make the jackpots bigger. Current odds are closer to 290 million to 1, and more bettors than ever are being attracted despite worse odds. If someone has lottery winnings as a retirement plan, he or she better have a good contingency. People do better to channel energy to catch what is possible—and forget what is not.

After finishing school, we pursue good jobs that challenge us, provide opportunities to learn and build a career, and compensate us. Preparing for such jobs generally involves securing a good education and demonstrating exemplary performance when given challenging tasks. It often involves

 Dogs like to chase cars, but they also like to ride in cars. Dave Barry, the comedian and author, once said, "Dogs feel very strongly that they should always go with you in the car, in case the need should arise for them to bark violently at nothing right in your ear."[3]

networking and obtaining access to those who make hiring decisions, particularly for the first job.

Achieving a successful career is usually reflected by advancement as measured by promotions and increasing levels of responsibility, peer recognition, and compensation. Chasing career success often requires changing jobs and relocating when more promising opportunities become available. It often involves sacrifices, hard work, long hours, and a commitment to excel.

Some people chase money. I have never found it productive to pursue money for the sake of making more money. In business, success generally provides increasing levels of compensation. The CEO of a company is paid considerably more than the typical worker for good reason: as employees advance and assume more leadership and responsibility, the money normally increases proportionally.

In my experience, people who are focused solely on money often miss out on the many nonfinancial rewards that come from chasing and catching other goals, such as a successful family life. Studies have shown that money does not translate into happiness.[4] It is better to have money than be poor, but I seem to meet lots of unhappy rich people who struggle with overly entitled children, unhappy spouses, and an insatiable desire to acquire more stuff. Benjamin Franklin, one of the US Founding Fathers, is known for advising thrift; he said, "A penny saved is a penny earned." But he also advised, "Money has never made man happy nor will it. There is nothing in its nature to produce happiness. The more of it one has, the more one wants."[5]

**I have never found it productive to pursue money for the sake of making money.**

Some pursue or chase fame and the recognition (and possibly adulation) associated with fame. Such recognition and attention certainly can boost self-image and ego, but there are pitfalls even for those who achieve fame. Because of media focus, celebrities often become aware of their perceived shortcomings and may be driven to depression or self-destruction. They can become overly self-conscious and may need to deal with a loss of status if their fame diminishes. One psychologist equates the wish for fame as a "crippling, undiagnosed malady."[6]

Pursuit of nonbusiness careers is often not as rewarding financially, but it provides other rewards. Teachers, for example, are rewarded with the knowledge that they have helped children learn and prepare for their future. Teachers, nurses, social workers, and many other professionals work in jobs that bring mental and emotional satisfaction from helping others; that can translate into career success. For these professionals, success is not measured in terms of money.

Nurses typically work long hours attending patients in pain. Some patients suffer from incurable conditions, and the nurses must remain positive and encouraging while knowing their patients will almost certainly die. The nurses I have met, including my niece Jackie, are driven by the desire to help others and not just the paycheck. The rest of us benefit from this attitude of service.

In managing organizations, as in life generally, beware of what you chase because you may catch it.

Cooper, the small, white Goldendoodle, loves to chase balls and almost everything else. On the beach, Cooper tries to chase balls with the big dogs like Beau and Rosie but is not successful. His legs are too short, and he cannot run as fast. Cooper realized, however, that when the big dogs return with the balls, they drop them at their owners' feet so the owners can pick the balls up and throw them again. Now Cooper hangs around the owners, grabs the ball after the bigger dog drops it and before the owner can pick the ball up, and runs around the beach, displaying his successful chase for all to see. To win the race or successfully complete the chase, one needs to be creative and use his or her special talents like Cooper does.

If one initiates a partnership or joint venture, he or she must be truly prepared to operate with a partner and give up sole decision-making. What happens when the partners disagree?

In business, everyone wants access to capital. For small businesses, this usually means a financial partner to provide funding for business initiatives. Many executives seem to complain, however, when the financial partner intervenes in the decision-making. If someone takes the money, they should be ready to share the decision-making.

If a new business strategy is established, are the resources available to make it a success? If a business segment is being expanded, is the company prepared to terminate other business segments and lay off or retrain employees to make capital available for the new venture?

Business and management involve lots of chasing and, if successful, catching. The biggest chases are often corporate acquisitions and mergers. Chasing and capturing other companies or organizations through mergers and acquisitions are especially popular with investors and analysts. In my experience, however, the acquiring companies often appear to overstate cost savings and operational synergies from acquiring another company and fail to recognize the challenges of merging systems, cultures, and people. This can lead to optimistic forecast future earnings. However, acquisitions can also demonstrate executive leadership and vision, if the deal makes sense, and virtually all transactions provide onetime opportunities for the acquiring company to manage its future earnings through creative but permitted accounting techniques.

There are many examples of companies chasing and catching big companies (like Sadie's cars). Sometimes, catching the car does not work out so well despite the pursuing company's good intentions and presumed logic.

In 1998, Daimler, owner of Mercedes-Benz, purchased Chrysler for about $37 billion. My last car was a Mercedes. The company makes wonderful cars, but its leaders made a bad business decision to chase Chrysler. Reportedly, they sought to become an automobile giant to compete with other big car companies like General Motors and Toyota.

**The acquiring company receives the applause, but the selling company gets the money.**

Eight years later, Daimler paid a private equity group $650 million to take ownership of Chrysler. The synergies between luxury Mercedes automobiles and midmarket Chrysler cars never materialized.

Sometimes, once a company has completed successful acquisitions, its management becomes convinced all of its acquisitions will be successful. Hewlett-Packard, or HP, the prominent computer company, has had a long history of successful corporate acquisitions. I like HP. I own a HP printer, my former company used HP servers, and I own a few shares of their stock. However, in 2011 they purchased the technology firm Autonomy for about $11 billion. In 2015, only four years later, HP formally wrote off $8.8 billion of the $11 billion purchase price. The overvaluation apparently stemmed from Autonomy's use of aggressive and possibly illegal accounting techniques, which inflated revenues and earnings. The acquisition was a major blunder and greatly tarnished HP's record.

Closer to home, in late 2014, Haggen, a small grocery store chain consisting of 18 stores based in Bellingham, Washington, agreed to purchase 164 grocery stores from Safeway, mostly in California, including the Albertsons store I shopped at near my home. The stores were bought and rebranded between March and June 2015; I remember when the new sign appeared at my store. A few months later, on September 8, 2015, Haggen filed for bankruptcy and closed almost all of the newly acquired stores, including the one near me. Haggen apparently underestimated marketing requirements and sales-building strategies in the highly competitive southern California markets. When sales did not meet expectations, the company cut expenses instead of increasing marketing. This led to a death spiral with poorer service, higher prices, and less marketing. Haggen's acquisition demonstrated a level of corporate and executive incompetence rarely witnessed, in my judgment.

There are also many examples of successful mergers and acquisitions that were able to realize synergies and greater efficiencies. In 2008, the two satellite radio companies Sirius and XM Radio merged. Both were losing money, but together they were able to reduce duplicative costs, operate more efficiently, and market a single product to the automobile industry.

In 2000, the well-regarded investment bank J. P. Morgan merged with the well-known and highly regarded retail bank, Chase Manhattan. J. P. Morgan's strengths were in investment banking, private banking for companies and high-net-worth individuals, and wealth and asset management. Chase Manhattan operated a large retail branch banking business and was one of the nation's largest credit card processing operations.

Together, the banks offered a full array of services and diversified their capital sources and income generation. It has been a successful merger. Today J. P. Morgan Chase is the largest bank in the United States and one of the largest corporations in the world.

Studies have shown that catching or acquiring another company is usually most beneficial to the owners or investors in the company that was acquired. The acquiring company receives the applause, but the selling company gets the money.

Making more money and acquiring stuff is the human equivalent to a dog catching balls. If one chooses a career that does not compensate financially, achieving personal satisfaction and fulfillment is catching the ball. Creating a successful life and family is catching the rabbit. Don't waste time chasing cars or unachievable dreams.

### Chapter Takeaways

1. One must be careful what one chooses to pursue.
2. Be realistic in the quest.
3. Have a plan of what to do in case of success.

# 12

# Earning Trust and Choosing Partners

© Martin Bucella. Used with permission.

*At first after moving to California, I was always on the leash. Now I run free on the beach, in a big nearby park, and wherever there are no cars. Scott trusts me to come when called.*

*One of my neighbors, Zug, a golden retriever, used to go to the beach with me. Zug loves the ocean and often goes in for a swim but does not come out when called. One time Zug made his owner wait two hours while he played in the water. Now Zug's owner won't let him go to the beach anymore because she does not trust him to come when called.*

*I learn a lot of useful things when I hang out with other, friendly dogs. For example, Jake, a big Bernese mountain dog, taught me how to pee like a male dog, and he also taught me how to scratch the ground after a poop. I looked* up to Jake and trusted him, so I just copied what he did. Scott doesn't like it when I scratch after poops, because I tend to send poop pieces flying. A few times I hit Scott with a flying poop when he bent down to pick it up, but now he knows to stand clear until I am done.

I am careful whom I choose to play with. For example, nobody wants to play with Bucky, the ball thief. Bucky is a young English golden retriever. He likes to steal other dogs' balls and then play keep-away. When his owner threatens him unless he gives up the ball, Bucky runs into the ocean beyond his owner's reach. Finally, someone bribes Bucky with a treat, and he gives up the ball; it is hard to eat with a ball in your mouth.

When you pick the wrong partner, you can acquire bad habits too. Bucky's friend Radar learned how to steal balls by watching Bucky. Now I have to watch out for both dogs.

Rosie and I are good partners, especially when Rosie is not chasing balls. Whenever I find something good to eat on the beach, Rosie will run over and join in the feast. When Rosie finds something with a big odor, I will often run over and roll in it. We help each other and share when we find good things.

Some people are givers; they obtain satisfaction by giving to others and making others happy. They make the best dog owners. Other people are takers; they are most happy when they receive things. They enjoy being licked by an affectionate dog but complain when they have to take us on walks or clean up our messes. Everyone should beware of partnering with a taker.

Dogs are pack animals; we inherently rely on our fellow pack members. Collectively, we are stronger and have more fun as long as we choose our pack members carefully. Beau, Rosie, me, and our owners and my neighbor Shirley are a pack; we walk together and look out for each other.

Some dogs are more trustworthy than others, and it is important to pick friends and playmates carefully. If you invite the wrong dog over, he will eat your breakfast when you are not looking.

\* \* \*

One of my favorite sayings is "Players score points, but teams win games." If you want your organization to succeed, surround yourself with team players who support each other, and avoid self-proclaimed "stars." A team is not unlike a dog pack. Working together makes everyone better. Casey Stengel, the iconic manager of the New York Yankees and the New York Mets, once said, "Finding good players is easy. Getting them to play as a team is another story."[1]

Rosie loves to chase and catch balls. Bru is older Labrador mix and chases balls too, but Bru is no longer fast. When Bru's owner, Betsy, flings Bru's tennis ball on the beach, sometimes Rosie catches it instead of Bru. Rosie's owner, Rick, then has to give the ball back to Betsy and apologize for Rosie stealing Bru's ball. One day Rosie figured out this situation was not working; she still caught Bru's ball, but instead of returning it to Rick, she returned it to Bru, who returned it to Betsy. This was great teamwork: Betsy to Rosie to Bru to Betsy. Everyone benefited from the teamwork.

Martin Luther King Jr. once said in a speech, "We may have all come in different ships, but we're in the same boat now. Working together to row the boat is the only sure way forward."[2]

## Players score points, but teams win games.

Partnerships in the animal world almost certainly pre-date human partnerships. Like in so many other areas, humans can learn from others in the area of partnership. Many animals rely on partnerships to succeed where they would fail if acting alone. Snow geese typically fly five thousand miles between the Arctic and the southern United States and other areas equally distant each year. They fly in a V formation to minimize wind resistance. The lead geese, which experience the most wind resistance, trade off positions with those that use less energy in the back positions. By working as a team, the geese can fly great distances at exceptional speeds without many stops.

The emperor penguin breeds in the harsh Antarctic winter. The female lays the egg, which is incubated by the male while the female searches for food. Then the parents trade off on searching for food and protecting the egg. If either parent does not find food or keep the egg warm, it will not hatch. If either parent strays from his or her monogamous relationship and briefly leaves the egg unprotected, the embryo dies. This parenting requires teamwork and extreme dedication.

Sibe was an eight-year-old German shepherd who lived on a farm in Texas. Every Sunday all the relatives gathered for dinner. Often everyone came early and went to the distant part of the farm where the big pecan trees grew. Grandparents, parents, and children all gathered the nuts and walked back through the bushes on the long path, always on the lookout for poisonous snakes and wild animals. One Sunday, someone noticed after the family returned that five-year-old Felicia had not returned with the group and was missing. The men went out through the fields, but their search was unsuccessful. Amid the angst and fear, about twenty minutes later, seven-year-old Tommy started yelling as loud as he could, "Look, there's Sibe! He is pulling Felicia by her dress." Sibe's role in the family was to protect the children, including Felicia. When Felicia became separated from the others, Sibe found her and pulled her back to the main house step by step.

Humans and dogs also have a history of working together as a team, including under extreme conditions. Near Anchorage, Patti and I recently watched the start of the Iditarod Trail Dog Sled Race with our friends Marcia and Rick Gold. The Iditarod race is probably the most challenging sporting event in the world, with dog sled teams and their human mushers traveling across Alaska over one thousand miles in extreme cold and often blizzard conditions. The human driver and his or her dogs rely on each other to survive in the most unhospitable conditions imaginable. The fastest time in history took more than eight days, and often teams work for two weeks before finishing the grueling contest.

Like in Sadie's world, trust is important in all relationships and situations. Educational policy expert Megan Moran wrote a well-known book titled *Trust Matters: Leadership for Successful Schools*. She describes three principals in schools with predominantly low-income students; each one has a different leadership style. She concludes that the most successful result is achieved by the principal who is able to create a climate of trust between teachers, students, and families.[3] This matches Patti's experience as a principal.

Work environments are often improved when employees share tasks and duties. My niece Jackie works with two nursing assistants who change beds, give patient baths, and provide for patient comfort. Instead of working separately, they began working as a team and quickly discovered they worked faster together and had more fun talking to each other as they worked. Jackie refers to the strategy as "combine and conquer."

Often partnerships work for a while, but then conditions change, and the same partnership is no longer as satisfactory. We are accustomed to musical groups splintering—like Guns N' Roses, the Everly Brothers, the Smashing Pumpkins, the Eagles, and even the Beatles. Breakups in the entertainment industry in Hollywood and New York seem to happen regularly too—Steven Spielberg and Amy Irving, Ben Affleck and Jennifer Garner, Jennifer Aniston and Brad Pitt, and more recently Angelina Jolie and Brad Pitt.

What we typically do not anticipate is the breakup of our own partnership or marriage, which happens with increasing frequency. In the United States, about 50 percent of marriages end in divorce. A recent trend of long-term marriages terminating in divorce also appears evident, especially for adults aged fifty or older.[4]

After my divorce following thirty years of marriage, my good friend Tom McCarthy counseled me, "Things will get better; they always do." He had suffered from a divorce and then benefited from falling in love and marrying his second wife, Kathy. Subsequently, I met Patti, and my life has indeed improved significantly. Tom's advice was worth remembering.

There are many examples of successful partnerships in virtually every industry. The entertainment industry has numerous examples of two professionals teaming up to achieve greater success than they could have achieved alone. The comedians Laurel, an Englishman, and Hardy, an American from Georgia, were paired in 1927 and made over one hundred popular films together. William Abbott and Lou Costello paired in 1935 and worked onstage together for more than twenty successful years. Desi Arnaz and Lucille Ball married in 1940 and worked together to create one of the most popular television series of all time, *I Love Lucy*. Prior to becoming partners, neither achieved nearly the success they did together.

Similar partnership successes have occurred in ballet (Margot Fonteyn and Rudolf Nureyev), dance (Fred Astaire and Ginger Rogers), movies (Katharine Hepburn and Spencer Tracy), and music (Richard Rogers and Oscar Hammerstein), to list a few examples. Consider the thousands of films

Nanuk was never fond of his cat roommate, Tinkerbelle. The gray tiger cat liked to sleep in Nanuk's favorite sunny places, easily hopped up on places Nanuk could not reach, and sometimes taunted Nanuk from fence tops or low branches of trees in Nanuk's yard. But Nanuk somehow figured out how to work with Tinkerbelle. Whenever the cat jumped on to the kitchen countertop, Nanuk was quick to enter the kitchen and convince Tinkerbelle to knock packages of food onto the floor, where Nanuk could tear them open and eat the contents. Sometimes you have to partner with someone you don't like to accomplish what you cannot achieve alone.

and artistic performances that did not result in enduring partnerships, and the importance of choosing the right partner becomes apparent.

In sports, the Chicago Bulls improved significantly when they added Michael Jordan to their team in 1984, but it was not until they added Scottie Pippen that they began to win championships. In professional tennis, brothers Bob and Mike Bryan were consistently ranked the number one men's doubles team in the world, but neither achieved similar success as an individual player.

In business, there are many examples of successful partnerships. In 1892, the brothers Orville and Wilbur Wright opened a bicycle shop together in Dayton, Ohio. Bored with bicycles and intrigued with the possibility of flight, the brothers invented an airplane and flew it at Kitty Hawk, North Carolina. This was the first time a manned airplane actually flew, and its success led to the development of commercial airplanes.

Technology has been the beneficiary of partnerships. Bill Hewlett and David Packard founded Hewlett-Packard after they graduated from Stanford in 1934. Working from a garage in Palo Alto, they first invented particular sound equipment and subsequently went on to become a leading supplier of computers and printers. Incidentally, the order of the name, Hewlett-Packard, was decided by a coin flip in 1939. Bill Gates and Paul Allen formed Microsoft in 1975, and Steve Jobs and Steve Wozniak founded Apple in 1976. In 1998, Larry Page and Sergey Brin started Google after meeting while working on their doctorates at Stanford University.

Successful business partnerships are not limited to technology companies. Ben Cohen and Jerry Greenfield, for example, formed Ben & Jerry's ice cream in Burlington, Vermont, in 1978. They first met in their seventh-grade gym class in Merrick, New York.

Not all partnerships are successful, and some are even disastrous for the participants. There are many hugely expensive divorces when spouses part ways, including Robert Murdoch's divorce from his third wife, Wendi Deng, which is rumored to have ended with a settlement of $1.7 billion. Jennifer Lopez reportedly paid backup dancer Cris Judd $14 million in a divorce settlement after only eight months of marriage.

Choosing the wrong business partners can be financially problematic. Noted sports stars have made millions of dollars during their careers but invested poorly with partners and advisors and lost everything. Bill Buckner, the all-star infielder for the Boston Red Sox and Chicago Cubs, filed for bankruptcy in 2008 when his auto dealership failed. Terrell Owens, the NFL star, filed for bankruptcy due to poor investments despite being paid $80 million during his playing career. Kenny Anderson earned $63 million while playing in the NBA but was forced to file bankruptcy in 2005 due to financial losses.[5]

In business, dealing with reputable, trustworthy partners is essential to achieving success and reducing the likelihood of loss. Many believe that hiring lawyers or accountants will protect them from financial loss even if the partners are questionable. Good advisors can certainly help in selecting investment partners and evaluating proposals, but they do not provide full protection.

---

## Dealing with reputable, trustworthy partners is essential to achieving success.

---

In business, whenever a deal goes bad, the respective parties call their lawyers to look at the applicable contract. The documentation is often voluminous. Sometimes I think lawyers get paid by the pound of documentation.

Across many deals, in my experience, the process is similar. The respective lawyers are first encouraging but also reflect uncertainty: "You are right, and we should prevail, but the judge could disagree." And it will cost considerable expense and time to obtain an answer.

The way to avoid such expense and uncertainty is to make deals with trustworthy partners who will do the right thing and not focus on documents. Picking the right partners is more important than documenting the deals, although documentation still is required and may be important.

Choosing the right attorneys is important too. I have benefited greatly by taking the advice of my long-term friends and attorneys Gene Pinover, in New York, and Mike Pruter, in San Diego. They are both problem solvers as opposed to problem dwellers.

If considering hiring a lawyer, ask for his or her experience and fees—and whether he or she has a dog. I find dog owners are often trustworthy, although non–dog owners can be trustworthy also. Unless the candidate answers the questions satisfactorily, one may want to interview some others before deciding. A number of years ago, I shook hands on a deal with Chuck Stevinson for a joint venture on a property just west of Denver, Colorado. We never documented the deal, but we both knew that if conditions worked out, we would develop the property together. After Chuck died, his son, Greg, took over the deal and honored the handshake. The bond between the parties was stronger than any legal document, but this was hard to explain at times to the corporate legal and accounting departments of my company.

Another deal, also in Denver, stands in stark contrast to my dealings with the Stevinsons. One night, I was sitting at a blackjack table in a Las Vegas casino where the International Council of Shopping Centers convened for its annual convention. I heard my name paged, which was a surprise; normally casinos are not looking for small bettors. "Yes," I answered on the white wall phone. "Scott, this is John from Detroit. I called to tell you that your project in the southeast of Denver will never be built. You should stop working on that project for your own sake and reputation." John was representing a big company and not threatening physical harm (at least I didn't think so) but was warning me of his company's intention to kill the proposed development of Park Meadows Shopping Mall, regardless of the cost and required tactics. The company did subsequently manage to delay the project by paying nearby residents to protest and by filing specious lawsuits. Eventually Park Meadows was built, but after that, I never considered doing a deal with the guys in Detroit; that was more than thirty years ago.

Many years ago, while I was at the Hahn Company in California, I was negotiating a deal with prospective partners in Minnesota. Ernie Hahn, a mentor and a legendary leader during the early days of the shopping center industry, accompanied me to the final negotiation meeting. Ernie made a few concessions we did not have to make, and I asked him later to explain. "Scott," he said, "always leave a few nickels on the table. That way they will appreciate your fairness and come back for another deal." Years later I was advising an executive with Morgan Stanley on negotiations with investors in Mexico. At one break, I told the Morgan Stanley guy to give the Mexican investors back a couple minor deal points that had already been won. "Why would I do that?" he asked in complete surprise.

"Because," I said, "they need to make some profit, and you always want to leave a few nickels on the table."

---

## If you're considering hiring a lawyer, ask for his or her experience and fees—and whether he or she has a dog.

---

If one ever needs to know if a prospective business partner is desirable, one should ask how many deals he or she did with former partners. If the prospective partner did only one deal with previous partners, then he or she is probably not someone to do business with. Good partnerships almost always lead to subsequent, additional ventures.

One of the most difficult negotiations I ever had was with Steve Furnary, who was managing partner of the New York asset-management firm Clarion Partners. Steve's pension fund client had specific requirements, and my company had different requirements that were incompatible. However, doing a deal and bringing the two companies together was otherwise very desirable. It was a very difficult negotiation, but we finally found a way to get the deal done. Steve and I went on to do other deals because we trusted each other.

I worked on many deals through the years with Morgan Stanley's Real Estate Funds group. In complex deals, there is always considerable opportunity for interpretation of documents and even amounts owed. The Morgan Stanley executives, such as Chris Niehaus and John Buza, were always fair in any issue that could be interpreted in different ways. For that reason, I returned to Morgan Stanley and its Real Estate Funds group many times to help on deals and with companies in which the company had an investment. Subsequently, Chris Niehaus and several of his colleagues joined former Morgan Stanley executive Sonny Kalsi at a new firm, Green Oak, that embodies the same attitude of trust and fairness.

Life and work are better with a partner than without, but only if you pick the right partner. Choose carefully—because the consequences of a wrong choice can be devastating.

### Chapter Takeaways

1. Choosing the right partner is more important than anything else, both in life and in business.
2. Players score points, but teams win games.
3. One can achieve greater success with the right partner than by relying on individual effort.

*My toy!*

# 13

# Eat, Sleep, Play

© Martin Bucella. Used with permission.

***My priorities are pretty clear.*** *I like to eat, I take long naps, and I like to play. I also like to hang out with my owner.*

*My first priority is to eat. Animals need to eat to survive, and animals everywhere concentrate first on finding food. In the wild, sometimes it can be difficult to find food. I know because my mom and I used to live in the wild.*

*At my home now, I don't have to hunt for my basic meals—they are delivered to my bowl twice a day.*

*When dogs have had enough to eat, we typically stop eating. I don't want to overeat, because it slows me down and makes me vulnerable.*

I don't overeat, but I am always on the lookout for a few good snacks. Once I approached a postal worker and begged her for food despite Scott's protest. She turned and produced a very tasty dog biscuit. Just this morning, another postal worker was walking by and delivered another treat when I begged. I like postal workers.

Dogs are not very particular about what we eat. I like going to human restaurants such Pacifica Breeze in Del Mar and Café 222 in San Diego. Sometimes I go with Scott for breakfast, and he feeds me bacon under the table, which tastes wonderful. I never get bacon at home. Dogs eat almost anything, but nothing beats the taste of crispy bacon.

My second priority is sleep. Dogs tend to sleep a lot. I like to sleep.

I rise early every morning, wake Scott up if he is not moving fast enough, and go for a long walk and run on the beach. Then I am served breakfast, and afterward I take a nap. If Scott goes out for coffee midmorning, I tag along, beg for snacks at Starbucks, and then return home and take another nap. We usually go out for other walks, followed by naps and dinner at five o'clock. This is how my day usually goes. Sleep, exercise and play, eat, and more sleep.

My third priority is play. I like to chase other dogs and be chased. I also like to play tug-of-war, keep-away, and fetch. Life without play would be boring.

It is important to pick the right friends and playmates; otherwise, even the most fun activities will not be that satisfying. I love to play tug-of-war. Beau and I play all the time. She grabs my leash, or I grab hers, or we both grab a rope toy, and we tug and growl. We are pretty evenly matched, so it's lots of fun. Cooper is good at tug-of-war too.

I played tug-of-war with Titan once. He is a Bernese mountain dog and is much bigger than I am. He just sat there when I tugged on his leash. I could not budge him no matter how hard I pulled. It wasn't that much fun.

I also played tug-of-war with Bhodie, who is a little dog. I dragged the poor guy all over the driveway. When he sat down, I dragged him until his mom, Vicki, intervened. It wasn't fun for him, but I really enjoyed it.

I also like to play keep-away. Chewy is good at keep-away. The other day I found a cool stick and was trying to keep it away from Chewy, but Bailey, a stocky yellow Lab, managed to take the stick away from me and broke it into pieces with his heavy jaws. Then he ate the stick. I am not playing keep-away with Bailey again.

*In addition to eating, sleeping, and playing, I enjoy spending time with Scott and Patti. I love to sit or lie beside them, especially at night in bed or during the day on the big living room couch that I am not supposed to be on. I also like to go for walks and just hang out.*

\* \* \*

We humans definitely have an eating problem. More than one-third of adult Americans are obese, and more than two-thirds are overweight or obese.[1] Obesity rates for adults have doubled since 1980. This affects employee health and productivity.

The trend of becoming overweight is apparent in children too. Childhood obesity rates have tripled since 1980. Seventeen percent of children are obese, and about one in three is overweight or obese.

To determine how an individual's weight compares, one simple tool that is available is the body mass index, or BMI, calculator. The calculator can be easily found on the internet or at the website cdc.gov. My BMI is 25.3; that means I am overweight. I know I am overweight because I have relatively good vision and can see what looks back at me in the mirror. But I enjoy eating good food, and dieting is difficult. Maybe tomorrow I will start a real diet.

When I do diet, the only system that works for me is writing down everything I consume and the related calories. Writing down what I eat forces me to recognize how much food and how many calories I consume, and this makes it easier to cut back. There are computer apps that make recording weight and consumption fairly easy, and I recommend this discipline. Eating one hundred fewer calories a day translates into ten pounds' weight loss in one year!

---

## One in three Americans suffers from high blood pressure.

---

People who are significantly overweight incur more health-related problems on average than people who are not fat. Type 2 diabetes has been linked to obesity and inactivity as well as other factors. An estimated twenty-nine million Americans have diabetes, and another eighty-six million have prediabetes. If these trends continue, one in three Americans will likely have diabetes someday. The current estimated medical cost to treat diabetes

## Gary's Guide to Eating

My friend Gary, who lives in Houston, once shared his theory on how to reduce calories. I have found no medical expert who concurs with Gary, but Gary was always in pretty good shape, so I thought I would pass along his thoughts.

1. If you break something like a cookie into two pieces, some calories escape into the air. Breaking a cookie into multiple pieces and eating one piece at a time is most effective.
2. If you eat a piece of fruit or vegetable, that helps neutralize the bad stuff you also eat. Eating a banana with breakfast, for example, can help offset the bad effects of the donut.
3. Drinking lots of water causes weight loss. Evidently, the water washes calories out before they have time to collect in the body.
4. Eating while standing or walking makes it harder for calories to accumulate than eating while sitting. Eating "on the run" could be particularly effective.

is about $245 billion per year in out-of-pocket medical expenses and lost productivity.[2]

One in three Americans suffers from high blood pressure, a leading cause of stroke. High blood pressure is the result of multiple factors, including genetics. But a sedentary lifestyle, excess weight, and an unbalanced diet are frequently associated with high blood pressure and can exacerbate unfavorable genetic dispositions. Stroke costs in the United States are estimated to be approximately $34 billion annually and rising.[3]

A stroke killed my father when he was only forty-seven years old, and I suffered a ministroke (a TIA) several years ago. The cost of strokes and other medical maladies far exceeds the financial calculations depicting the cost of treatment. The real cost to families and friends is much higher, as strokes can result in death or disability, resulting in poor quality of life and functioning.

What someone eats—and how much—definitely affects his or her health. Most dogs have a key advantage over humans with respect to eating. Dogs typically digest their food quickly, so they know when they are full and can stop eating. Humans have more complex digestive systems, and it often takes fifteen to thirty minutes for the receptors in the brain to receive the signal that a person is full. So, typical humans may continue eating even if they are full, because their brains do not know they are full. Dogs are much quicker to adjust than people.

Unlike dogs, we humans eat more than we appear to need or want. At dinner parties, I often hear people complain, "I am stuffed, but I think I will have . . ." I confess I have done this myself. If we are stuffed, why do we eat more?

As humans gain weight, we struggle to adjust. Losing weight is one of the greatest human challenges. Smoking is bad, but one can quit smoking entirely. Alcohol and drug addiction are terrible, but it is possible to stop. By contrast, it is not possible to stop eating and live. Cutting back eating is like trying to cut back slightly on smoking or drinking; it does not work well.

The other day, I chatted with an Uber driver who told me he only drives part time. His primary vocation is writing books on diet and nutrition, including weight loss. "What's the secret to losing weight?" I asked.

"Eat less," he replied.

That seems like a pretty good summary of the many diets that are promoted.

---

### Dog Food Diet

A customer tells the story of waiting in line at his local Walmart with a fifty-pound bag of dog food when the woman in line behind him asked if he was buying the food for his dogs. He thought this was a really stupid question and hesitated before responding, "No, actually I'm on the dog food diet. I just carry around a small bag of dog food, and anytime I get hungry, I eat a handful. Works great! Last time I lost thirty pounds, but I ended up in the hospital for a week." By then, everyone in line was listening, including the woman who asked the dumb question. She said, "Oh my God, what happened? Did you get sick from all the dog food?" Without cracking a smile, the man responded, "Nope. I was sitting in the road licking myself when I got hit by a car." Everyone in line broke out laughing, and the woman stormed off.[4]

Programs that completely change and regulate dietary intake, such as restricting consumption to specific prepared and packaged meals, can lead to significant weight loss. But when the controlled diet ends, the excess weight often returns.

Continued overeating may lead to poor health, premature death, and unaffordable medical expenses for individuals and the country's medical system. We need to emulate dogs' eating and exercise behavior in this regard, but it is challenging to do so. I know I need to eat less, eat better, and exercise more; however, it is difficult to do so when schedules are busy and time is constrained. And eating good food and drinking good wine are some of life's great pleasures.

In companies, having overweight managers and employees may lead to a loss of productivity and underperformance if health issues arise. However, losing weight is difficult. I have been trying to lose several pounds for months without success. Just cutting back on a few calories each day and adding some exercise does not seem to work. I once incentivized a manager to lose weight by paying a financial bonus for each pound lost. It worked for a while, but he eventually gained back the weight, which is not unusual. Some companies pay for annual physicals and have medical insurance that covers healthy lifestyle consultations, but employees and managers often need to be encouraged to take advantage. Some employers have on-site gyms or offer gym memberships as a benefit. Other employers offer other health-related benefits, such as Glendale Adventist Medical Center near Los Angeles, California, which offers employees access to Weight Watchers with on-site meetings and full reimbursement of expenses. Corporate leaders need to try alternatives and set the example to address this difficult problem.

In 2015, the life expectancy of Americans declined for the first time in almost twenty years, according to the Centers for Disease Control and Prevention. The increased death rate was attributed to increased heart disease related to obesity. Across all countries, the United States ranks thirtieth in life expectancy, similar to Cuba and Costa Rica and lagging behind many European and Asian countries, according to the World Health Organization.[5]

In addition to maintaining a proper weight, obtaining sufficient sleep is important for both dogs and people. We humans do not get enough sleep. Between stress and long hours at work, family and child-raising demands, and the demands of normal life, it is often sleep time that loses out. We often take drugs—mostly caffeine—to keep us awake. I rely on a big cup of

Starbucks coffee almost every morning. Dogs don't need drugs to sleep, but their lives are so much simpler.

The National Institutes of Health (NIH) reports that adults typically need seven and one-half to nine hours of sleep per night for optimal performance, but most adults report receiving only six to seven hours of sleep. According to the NIH, losing even one hour of sleep a night affects the ability to think properly and respond quickly.[6]

---

## Humans do not get enough sleep.

---

An article published by Everydayhealth.com suggests the first step in getting more sleep is to make sleep a priority.[7] WebMD reports that inadequate sleep causes at least ten problems:

- Sleepiness causes accidents.
- Sleep loss dumbs you down.
- Sleep deprivation can lead to serious health issues.
- Lack of sleep kills sex drive.
- Sleepiness is depressing.
- Lack of sleep ages your skin.
- Sleepiness makes you forgetful.
- Losing sleep can make you gain weight.
- Lack of sleep may increase risk of death.
- Sleepiness impairs judgment.[8]

Children require even more sleep. A one- to three-year-old child needs twelve to fourteen hours of sleep per day. A child between five and twelve years old requires ten to eleven hours of sleep each day.

Older adults often report changes in sleeping habits such as going to bed and/or arising earlier, lighter sleep, and waking up at night. Acquiring sufficient sleep is important for older adults because it improves concentration and memory and allows repair of damaged cells and the immune system.[9]

Naps can be one solution. Research studies have found that taking naps can be a good thing for rest, energy, blood pressure, and general health. However, naps that interfere with nightly sleep are not desired.[10]

According to the National Sleep Foundation, 85 percent of mammalian species are polyphasic sleepers. That means they sleep off and on during the day. Humans are in a minority because we try to sleep all at once. Perhaps this contributes to some people's sleep problems. A nap as short as five minutes can improve alertness. A nap of fifteen to forty-five minutes once a day evidently improves mood, alertness, and performance in humans.[11]

I have never been a good nap taker, but I sleep pretty well. My secret to sleeping is as follows:

1. Don't worry about sleep. Personally, I know I eventually will be sufficiently tired and fall asleep. If not tonight, then tomorrow night or the next night. Relax. The more you worry, the less you sleep.
2. Don't take sleep medication. It becomes a habit and eventually loses its potency, but the body doesn't lose its desire for more medications.[12]
3. When I am in bed but not sleeping, I rest. Resting is good for the body too, and when I am resting, I usually fall asleep.
4. Sometimes, I get out of bed and eat some cereal with milk. For some reason, that combination makes me sleepy.
5. If nothing else works, try reading something boring or tedious. I will often read part of an *Economist* magazine, which tires me quickly.
6. I also use a mouthpiece at night that pulls my jaw forward and inhibits snoring and irregular breathing. There may be a medical issue that contributes to sleep deprivation.

From a management perspective, employees and managers who do not sleep enough will not be as effective or productive as those who are well rested. Some policies to facilitate more rest include encouraging employees to avoid excess but unneeded work hours. Some corporate cultures reward employees for working late hours and having extended face time. I always arrived at work early but left in time to be home for dinner. I worked hard and productively when I was in the office and never felt the need to stay late unless there was a crisis or emergency situation, such as a big project under deadline. Rewarding late work hours, as a norm, results in a counterproductive culture that rewards work time instead of results.

Douglas Shackelford, dean of the prestigious Kenan Flagler Business School at the University of North Carolina, told me that they teach their MBA students that normal work hours provide benefits to the employee and the employer, in comparison to corporate cultures requiring consistently long work hours and excessive time in the office even when not required to complete tasks. He believes the primary reasons their MBA students are heavily recruited by companies throughout the United States are the students' work ethic, their attitude to teamwork, and their attitudes that balance life and work activities.

Providing access to counseling is also helpful if the lack of sleep is due to stress and worry about work or nonwork situations. Most company insurance includes such benefits.

Providing a professional work environment, free from harassment and unnecessary conflict, may also lead to a healthier life with less stress and fewer distractions. Communicating with employees within a company mitigates the stress of uncertainty and rumor. A team-based culture with collaborating employees generally results in greater corporate loyalty, better coworker support, and almost certainly less sleep-depriving stress.

In addition to proper eating and sufficient sleep, a third dog priority is play. Adults don't seem to play much. We watch others play, but it is rare to see humans running after each other. Some adults do run, and some ride bicycles, which are good activities for exercise but generally don't qualify as fun. For humans, exercise is often a type of work; for dogs, it is fun.

Walking, including taking dogs for a walk, is exercise and should be encouraged. But it is not the same as vigorous, heart-healthy exercise. Humans should emulate dogs and run if possible. If someone cannot run, he or she should swim, bike, dance, or use other aerobic exercises. When my knee became arthritic, and I could no longer run, I switched to an elliptical machine to maintain aerobic health and hopefully achieve a longer, healthier life. I have lived longer than my father, my grandfather, and my great-grandfather

Dogs and people can overdo play and even hurt themselves. They can also be too possessive of their things. Barkley, a cairn terrier who lives in Maryland, likes to pick up tennis balls and plays keep-away with other dogs in the park. One day, Barkley took a battered, soggy ball with him when he left the park and actually swallowed the ball. He made sure no other dog was going to get his prized ball. Unfortunately, the ball became stuck in his upper intestine, and Barkley had to have an operation to remove it.

despite our common genes. My doctor attributes my greater longevity to exercise and better available medical care.

Organizations can encourage playtime in a limited way. Many companies now provide showers and changing areas so employees can play ball or exercise at lunch or before or after work. I used to run at lunchtime in San Diego, where employees had access to locker rooms and showers, and I had many informative, productive discussions with colleagues who ran with me.

Organizations can also sponsor corporate activities such as an annual picnic, games, and family activities on occasion. At Investa, we had Friday afternoon snacks and drinks to close out the week, which did not provide much exercise but was a stress-free way to end the workweek. Our land development team bought a Ping-Pong table, and we often had spirited contests on Fridays after work. Employers will never be the source of most employee play and recreational activity, but introducing some fun makes the work more enjoyable and should lead to happier employees.

Among the keys to a happy, successful life are Sadie's recommendations: eat well but not too much, get lots of sleep, exercise, and have fun.

## Chapter Takeaways

1. Eat less.
2. Sleep more.
3. Play more.

# 14

# Being Loyal

© Martin Bucella. Used with permission.

**Every dog I know is loyal and faithful to its owner.** *I greet Scott every morning with a wagging tail, and I frequently jump with excitement when he climbs out of bed. I wait for him when we are out walking and he needs to stop. When he comes home at night, I am waiting for him, and when he watches TV, I curl up next to him.*

*I am also loyal to Patti, who gives me hugs and pets me and lets me snuggle next to her on the living room couch and the master bed. I would do anything for her; she is my friend.*

*Two years ago, my friend Titan's owner, Tom, became very sick. When he returned home to receive hospice care, Titan lay on the bed beside Tom every day from morning to night, leaving only occasionally to go to the bathroom, until Tom died a month later. Tom died knowing Titan was there to watch over him until the end.*

*Dogs are, by nature, loyal and faithful. My friend Beau is one of the most loyal and faithful dogs I know. When we walk on the beach in the morning, and Beau's owners Pat and Beth become separated, Beau will run back and forth, always checking on both of them. Actually, she checks on Beth because she wants Pat to keep throwing the tennis ball so Beau can fetch. When Beau catches the ball, she usually makes a big lap, returning to run by and check on Beth before returning to Pat so he can throw the ball again. Pat calls it Beau's victory lap after successfully catching the ball.*

*Rosie is loyal to Rick and Marcia. When Rick calls Rosie on the beach to go home, Rosie always comes, even though she would rather stay and play. Sometimes, she takes a few extra sniffs, hoping Rick will change his mind about leaving, but she always comes when he insists.*

\* \* \*

The word *loyalty* comes from a French word now translated as *legal*. Loyalty was once a legal concept. Subjects were loyal to the king; they were also legal subjects of the king. Today, loyalty refers more to mutual obligation and commitment. To be loyal in a relationship is to be faithful and supportive. To be loyal to one's family is to nurture, support, and assist whenever the need arises. To be loyal to friends is to be supportive no matter what the circumstances.

Bear lives with his owners (Scott's nephew and niece, Wade and Jackie) and a cat, Lupita, whom Bear tolerates. Lupita sometimes mocks Bear from places Bear cannot reach and acts like a typical self-absorbed, conceited feline. One day Wade and Jackie took care of a friend's big Irish wolfhound, who was at least twenty pounds heavier and several inches taller than Bear. When the giant dog lunged at Lupita, Bear intervened and forced the monster to back off. Bear may not have liked Lupita that much, but he was loyal and protective of his "sister." Loyalty to friends and family is the most important form of loyalty.

Loyalty and faithfulness are traits that lead to greater friendships and happier lives. If humans followed a dog's loyal example, we would be happier, healthier, and more successful.

Relationship counselors Linda and Charlie Bloom, authors of *Happily Ever After and 39 Other Myths about Love*, describe loyalty as a freely chosen commitment, rather than an obligation, which offers huge benefits to enhancing our lives.[1] They describe key characteristics of a loyal relationship between two partners:

- sexual fidelity
- spending time together, even if the activities are not always most desired
- taking the partner's side in disputes
- standing together in the face of adversity
- trying to see any disputed issue from the partner's perspective
- seeking a peaceful household by being less critical or judgmental
- listening to concerns
- carefully considering proposed agreements and honoring accepted agreements
- giving the benefit of the doubt
- helping the partner achieve what he or she desires
- celebrating successes
- focusing on the loyalty and forgiveness of the partner[2]

The loyalty of dogs is well known and often discussed. Alexander Pope, the noted English poet in the eighteenth century, once commented, "Histories are more full of examples of the fidelity of dogs than friends."[3] There is a common saying today: "If you live or work on Wall Street and want a friend, get a dog." In that competitive culture, dogs evidently make better friends than other humans.

 There are many comparisons of the loyalty and affection of dogs versus cats. As Christopher Hitchens writes, "Owners of dogs will have noticed that, if you provide them with food and water and shelter and affection, they will think you are God. Whereas owners of cats are compelled to realize that, if you provide them with food and water and affection, they draw the conclusion they are God."[4]

The loyalty of dogs has been recognized and appreciated for centuries.[5] The ancient temple of Gobekli-Tepe in Turkey shows clear evidence of domesticated family dogs around 12,000 BC. A grave from the same time frame in Israel had a man's body buried with a puppy, and dogs were prominently depicted in paintings from early Mesopotamia, the cradle of human civilization.

Dogs were companions to the ancient Goddess Inanna in the oldest known story from the Middle East, as documented in the *Epic of Gilgamesh* (2150–1400 BC). Dogs may have been around as long as humans.

The Roman goddess, Diana, was goddess of the hunt and was accompanied everywhere by her dogs. Similarly, Diana's Greek equivalent, the goddess Artemis, is often shown with symbols including the hunting dog.

---

## Do you remember who guarded the gates of Hades? Here's a clue. It wasn't a three-headed cat.

---

People have relied on dogs for companionship and other tasks like hunting for many centuries. When important humans died in ancient Egypt, they were often buried with their dogs to keep them company in their journey to the afterlife. The well-known Egyptian Pharaoh Ramses had pictures of dogs in his tomb and was buried with dogs.

If the dog lived with a rich Egyptian family, when it died, it was often mummified, buried, and sent on its way to the afterlife. This was recognition for the dog as a friend and trusted companion.

In ancient Greece, dogs frequently hung out with ancient deities. They also protected Greek gods and famous places. Do you remember who guarded the gates of Hades? Here's a clue. It wasn't a three-headed cat.

The concept of loyalty extends well beyond a dog's loyalty to its master. In organizations, employees owe their employer considerable loyalty. Employers are not required to hire a specific person or retain such a person. I have always felt that when a company hired and trusted me, it deserved my support and loyalty. If I ever felt it was no longer a good place to work, I was free to leave. But while I stayed and took the company's money, it deserved my allegiance.

At Investa, we had a young employee who did not have the proper work visa and was in danger of being forced to move back to her native Ireland.

There are countless stories of dogs that traveled great distances to find their owners. When the Dolan family of Aurora, Illinois, moved to East Lansing, Michigan, they gave their family dog, Tony, to friends in Aurora. Six weeks later, Tony showed up in East Lansing, 260 miles away, looking for his family.

Lazor, a three-year-old beagle, ran away when the fireworks started in Winnipeg Beach, Canada. His family was there on vacation and returned to their home fifty miles away without Lazor. He took some time to walk fifty miles, but Lazor showed up at his home a few weeks later despite the rugged terrain.

Moon, a Siberian husky, was lost seventy-seven miles from his home in Ely, Nevada. Moon crossed the desert, the White River, and the Ward Mountains to return to his owner in Ely.

There are many stories throughout history of dogs remaining loyal to their owners even after the owner's death. Canelo, a dog in Cadiz, Spain, used to accompany his owner to the local hospital where the owner received dialysis treatment. In 1990, the owner died, but Canelo waited outside the hospital for his owner for the next twelve years. There is now a street in Cadiz named after Canelo.

Hachiko, an Akita, has a statue in Tokyo. He waited at the train station for his master to return every day for nine years after his master's death.

Capitan, a German shepherd in Argentina, found his owner's grave in the local cemetery and remained there for almost ten years, standing guard and keeping company.

This situation was causing her considerable distress, but she lacked the resources to secure the proper visa. We decided to help and hired a firm specializing in obtaining work visas, at considerable expense to our company. I thought it was the right thing to do to help a good employee. We were able to secure the appropriate visa for her, but soon after, armed with an official work visa, she resigned and accepted another job elsewhere that paid slightly more money. There was no appreciation or consideration of the company's loyalty to her, and it caused us to consider whether we would make such an effort again in a similar situation.

Young people starting a career often learn at one job and jump quickly to another job. Giving their employer more loyalty for teaching and training would be desirable and represent a payback of sorts. Employees who are only focused on personal, short-term remuneration and show no organizational loyalty are like companies who are only focused on maximizing short-term profits at the expense of their employees. Neither will succeed over time as well as they otherwise would.

---

**Employees who are only focused on personal, short-term remuneration and show no organizational loyalty are like companies that are only focused on maximizing short-term profit at the expense of their employees.**

---

Employers owe their loyalty to their employees too. Organizational loyalty to employees takes several forms. Creating a professional and supportive environment for employees is the most basic requirement. Employees spend considerable time at their jobs and deserve to work in an environment that does not tolerate harassment, provides merit-based advancement opportunities and competitive compensation, provides employees access to job openings, and operates in an ethical atmosphere. Leadership in any organization should provide encouragement to its staff when times are challenging and should share the benefits in times of success. They should encourage team-based problem solving and company pride.

In addition to a professional work environment, employers should provide basic employee benefits. In the United States, such benefits include medical insurance, vacation days and sick time, and a retirement plan. Other countries typically require these benefits by law. The level of support provided by US organizations will vary with the financial capacity of the organization, but if an organization cannot even provide the most basic of benefits, it probably should not be in business. If an organization declines to provide benefits even if it could afford to do so, it is exploiting its employees and should not expect loyalty in return.

Lifestyle benefits are also part of showing loyalty to employees and are typically not costly. Some flexibility in working hours allows parents to drop off and pick up children at school or daycare. At Center America, we allowed employees to start and end work one hour before or after the normal work time, and it made a significant difference to several of our accountants who were working moms. The flexible-hours policy also created considerable corporate loyalty and resulted in less employee turnover. Likewise, flexibility in working from home on occasion is helpful, particularly if a working parent has a child or invalid parent at home and if the specific job does not require regular in-office contact. Policies to encourage additional learning and education can pay dividends in employee productivity. Employee morale-building events such as employee picnics, Friday after-work social hours, and pizza-for-lunch days create a positive work environment.

Many studies have shown the primary reason an employee stays at a job is not compensation. Although financial remuneration is important, most employees keep working for a company because they feel appreciated, enjoy the work environment, and feel treated well by the organization and their fellow employees. Organizational loyalty to employees is good business.

Linda, the receptionist of Center America in Houston, was a single mother. She was arrested outside the firm's office in 1995 for unpaid traffic tickets and was taken to jail. The company's general counsel used all available legal contacts and favors to locate Linda and post bail before she was to pick up her son from daycare later that day. Nothing else took priority in the company until Linda was free. She was an important team member, and the company owed her for her work effort and loyalty. Twenty years later, Linda was still working in the same office, helping new and old employees, and showing considerable loyalty to the company and staff who were loyal to her.

Loyalty to family, friends, partners, employees, and employers is important and rewarding. Think like a dog, and you will remain loyal to those you need and who need you.

### Chapter Takeaways

1. Be loyal to your family.
2. Be loyal to your employees, employer, and colleagues.
3. Loyalty makes life better.

Sadie waiting for Rosie to come out and play. © Peter Steusloff. Used with permission.

# 15

# Training People

© Martin Bucella. Used with permission.

**I have been to dog training.** *Humans talk a lot about dog training, but frankly I prefer to talk more about human training.*

*Dogs have done a pretty good job of training humans to feed us, take us for walks, throw balls, and clean up after us, but there is still more that people can learn. This is how I trained Scott.*

*First, it's important to know your subject. I know what Scott likes. For example, he likes to go for walks and chat with neighbors and friends, so he usually responds well when I suggest we go for a walk.*

*Providing what he likes gets better results than not doing what he enjoys. I have noticed that some people like licks, but others prefer just tail wags. Scott is okay with both but backs away if I lick too much. Patti likes licks better than Scott does.*

*The best training tools involve rewards. Rewards can be overt affection, praise, or food. I prefer food, but people seem to prefer affection. Always be generous with affection. When Patti asks if I want to go "walkee," I run to the door and wag my tail as fast as I can. This makes her happy and gets me more walks.*

*Complaints and growls are the least effective training tool. When someone yells at me for barking, for example, I often bark louder. When a dog I don't like walks by my house, I bark as loud as I can. Sometimes, Scott yells, "Shut up!" I interpret the yelling as him joining in the barking. If Scott offered me a treat instead of yelling, I would shut up quickly.*

---

## The best training tools involve rewards.

---

*Trust is important. No one should promise a treat and then not deliver one, for example. And no one should walk a dog with only dog biscuit crumbs in his or her pocket. We dogs can smell the crumbs and think we will get a real biscuit if we behave. Pretending to have something or offering the possibility of a treat and then not delivering is deceptive.*

*When a dog or person is not acting in an acceptable way, it is important to let him or her know right away. Bailey's owner, Teri, carries a can of compressed air that makes a loud, ear-splitting sound when released. Whenever Bailey plays too rough with another dog or vice versa, Teri uses this noise-maker to get everyone's attention and stop the undesired behavior. Dogs like me do not like loud noises, and Teri knows this.*

*Sometimes, humans put shock or electronic collars on dogs. I used to jump at and potentially knock down joggers or bicyclists. I was just playing, but my actions made everyone upset. Finally, Scott put a shock collar on me and buzzed me whenever I acted like I was about to go after a passing candidate. I quickly learned to stop jumping at joggers and bicyclists.*

*I think bad behavior is sometimes due to boredom and lack of exercise. If I am tired from running on the beach or in the park, I am more likely to be quiet and complacent than if I have been sitting all day. This morning I ran a lot, and now I am feeling like I need a long nap on the sofa.*

\* \* \*

There are many books, videos, and articles on dog training. There are even television programs on dog training. There is a big industry of dog trainers selling services to humans who own dogs. There are group training sessions and private, in-home training. But training dogs actually requires training people, according to Cesar Millan, the well-known "dog whisperer" and trainer. He says, "I rehabilitate dogs; I train people."[1]

Dogs do not understand English or whatever the human master uses as a language. Humans generally communicate in the same language, so it is easier for people to train other people. When training dogs and humans, however, keep the concept and words simple.

Training sessions should be short and focused. Both humans and dogs typically have trouble remembering multiple instructions or learning complex behavioral instructions. Cell phones and other talkative humans are not a problem for dogs but can easily distract humans, which interferes with their training sessions.

Training should begin at an early age. There is an old proverb, which apparently dates back to the 1500s and appeared in a book in the 1700s, that remains in wide use today: "You cannot teach old dogs new tricks."[2]

Nordstrom is famous for its customer service culture. Once, in a meeting with Jim Nordstrom, the CEO at the time, I asked about the company's employee training programs that led to such a successful culture. Jim replied,

If a dog runs away and subsequently returns, a human may be tempted to discipline the dog for running away. But if the discipline is administered after the dog returns, the dog will most likely think he or she is being disciplined for returning. Jack is a golden retriever who lives nearby behind an invisible electric fence. Sometimes he becomes frightened—like when there are fireworks—and he runs through the invisible fence. When he tries to return later after quiet is restored, he is shocked by the same electric fence. So, he typically goes wandering instead of returning home. Sometimes discipline can result in unexpected and unanticipated consequences for dogs and people, especially if the one disciplined does not understand why he or she is being punished.

"The training programs are not the key. When we hire an employee, they have already been trained for twenty years by their parents, and a week or two of an in-store training program won't make that much difference. The key," he said, "is hiring the right people to begin with."

Jim Nordstrom's philosophy was a more contemporary application of the philosopher Plato's observation, "The most important part of education is right training in the nursery."[3]

## Criticism does not typically result in desired behavior.

Training and altering behavior by using rewards has been widely known for many years, both in the dog world and human world. The Russian psychologist Ivan Pavlov became famous when he observed how dogs anticipated food when his assistant rang a bell. Psychologists are still talking about Pavlov's experiment over one hundred years later. Any dog could have predicted this. Ring a bell and give a dog food, and soon the dog will anticipate food when he or she hears the bell. This is not "rocket science," but we still seem fascinated to learn that rewards and anticipated rewards influence behavior.

Humans evidently learn more slowly than dogs. Even one hundred years after dogs taught Pavlov that rewards matter, people are still resorting to less effective tools to change behavior.

Some humans like to criticize others. Some people find things to criticize every day. Criticism does not typically result in desired behavior and more often actually causes undesired behavior, such as withdrawal or confrontation. Like dogs, humans who are criticized sometimes don't even understand why they are being criticized.

Excessive criticism can lead to abuse in a relationship. When one partner frequently criticizes or demeans another, it can result in poor self-image, low confidence, and feelings of failure and worthlessness in the criticized partner. It is generally caused by one partner trying to control and dominate the other through emotional abuse. Criticism and abuse are not training techniques and will not typically trigger the desired behavior.

Humans use punishment, including severe punishment for grievous actions. The worst offenders can be confined in prison. Incarcerating people is not a form of training. Prison removes people from society and from

While rewards are the preferred training tool, punishing bad behavior is sometimes necessary. For example, Rosie sometimes wears an antibark collar when she barks too much. When Rosie barks with her collar on, the collar releases citronella. Citronella does not harm her and causes no pain, but dogs hate the smell of citronella. It usually stops the barking.

Sometimes things do not work out as planned, however, including bark collars. One time when Rosie was riding with Rick in the car, the bark collar went off for no apparent reason, filling the car with citronella. Rosie tried to escape and went a bit berserk while Rick tried to drive the car filled with gas and a greatly animated and unhappy dog. Rick could not stop or open a window or Rosie would have bolted. Fortunately, Rick did not hit anyone as he navigated the way home.

doing more harm for a time, but the threat of prison does not seem to inhibit criminal actions. Like Sadie, I think it could be more effective if people who behave badly had to wear shock collars and were given a good buzz when they acted improperly. While punishment can be justified, it should be consistent with the gravity of the wrongful behavior and only attempted when treats and kindness do not succeed.

Some humans and dogs have psychological issues. Some dogs are timid and afraid while others are high strung and anxious. The same can be said for humans. It is hard to train someone who has other psychological issues. If a person is having problems, doctors often prescribe medications to help modify his or her behavior. Meds work for dogs too. Rosie is on Prozac, which has calmed her down considerably. Sometimes Beau and a couple of other dogs on the beach are given CBD (cannabidiol) or marijuana-derived oil externally to calm them during stressful times like the Fourth of July fireworks. If a human is acting irrationally, he or she may need medical attention and prescription drugs before any training can be effective.

Dogs and people can suffer from separation anxiety. When a human master is leaving the home, and the dog will remain home alone for an uncertain length of time, the dog starts worrying the human may not return. It is not unlike a child who doesn't want her mother to leave the home. Neither the dog nor the child has the knowledge or confidence to expect return of the master or parent. So, the child cries, and the dog barks and does other unacceptable activities like chewing on shoes and furniture. It is difficult to train someone if he or she is concerned about being abandoned or ignored. All training includes attention to communication.

Usually training involves instruction from those with greater knowledge and experience. The capability of the trainer or teacher will largely determine the effectiveness of any training. Teachers and training professionals can provide more effective training using tailored and organized communication techniques based on the experience of training others and knowing what methods are best suited to specific conditions and circumstances.

Schoolteachers are required to complete considerable education and training, including student teaching. They are constantly and formally evaluated as student teachers, new teachers, and even while employed. They are often required to pass tests and obtain certifications during their teaching careers.

In a recent research study conducted by economists at Harvard and Columbia Universities, having a good fourth-grade teacher results in a statistically greater chance that a student will go to college, not become a teenage parent, and make more money during his or her working life. Similarly, an ineffective teacher results in poor later-in-life performance.[4]

Like teachers, nurses receive considerable training in school and at work. Typically, new nurses are required to pass a ten-week supervised on-the-job training program after completing academic and licensing requirements. Only then is a nurse typically allowed to work on a floor unsupervised.

In business, I have often used outside experts to help solve problems, especially issues that require technical expertise. At Investa, we hired a technology consultant who uncovered many defects in our system. The consultant then helped us replace some of our technical staff, install new systems, and train staff in the new systems and procedures, which made us more productive. Had we relied on the original staff—who likely contributed to the problems—we would never have been able to improve our operations.

Every successful company I know has employee-training programs. I spent much of my career in the retail shopping center business. Retailers rely on in-store staff to present and sell their merchandise, but the companies are under pressure to keep costs low to remain competitive. Their only hope of success is to hire less-experienced staff and train them. The effectiveness of their staff hiring and training programs often determines whether a particular store will be successful.

One of the most successful retailers in the world is Starbucks. Howard Schultz, legendary founder and chairman of Starbucks, acknowledged the importance of training when he said, "Starbucks is not an advertiser; people think we are a great marketing company, but in fact, we spend very little money on marketing and more money on training our people than advertising."[5]

Everyone needs training, including people and dogs. Look for opportunities to train and be trained, but seek trainers and teachers who are professional and particularly good at what they do. Training requires consistency and setting boundaries. Proper training can improve the lives of all who participate.

## chapter Takeaways

1. Reward good behavior.
2. Rewards generally work better than criticism or punishment.
3. Choosing the right teacher is critical to learning.

TV can be boring.

# 16

## Everyone Needs a Job

© Martin Bucella. Used with permission.

*Everyone needs a job—a productive reason to exist. No dog is happy with an aimless, nondirected life. My primary job is to bark when someone approaches the house. I also wake up Scott in the morning if he shows signs of oversleeping for our morning walk. I give Scott and Patti lots of comfort and love, especially when they appear unhappy. I also clean up any food that falls on the floor. I am pretty busy working between naps and playtime.*

*Every dog I know has a job. Some dogs provide protection by barking when a stranger approaches the dog's owner. Rosie is good at scaring strangers away when on a leash with Rick, for example. Some dogs provide comfort and friendship like BJ, one of my neighbors, does for his owner, David. They are always out of town, traveling somewhere together. BJ has even been approved to travel in the passenger section of airplanes as a comfort dog. Some dogs, like Bucky, dig big holes on the beach so other dogs can play the "It's my hole" game.*

*My friend Titan is a hospice dog. He comforts people who are sick and likely to die. Titan is such a big, friendly dog—he could make anyone smile, even someone who is sick.*

*Beau, one of my best friends, protects her house from strangers and pests. One time she was relaxing in the backyard and discovered a rat in the compost pile. Beau tore through the entire pile—getting totally covered with compost and manure—and successfully chased the rat away. Her owner, Beth, was not pleased when Beau tried to reenter the house dripping with sludge. Sometimes people don't appreciate hard work, even in challenging environments, but lack of appreciation does not deter any conscientious dog from doing her job and doing it well.*

* * *

Dogs take on "real" jobs in addition to fun jobs like chasing balls or barking at UPS drivers. Dogs have been in the military for a long time. In the Revolutionary War, dogs helped out by carrying things. In World War I, the military used dogs to find and kill the rats that were plaguing the trenches. In World War II, dogs were used as messengers, scouts, sentries, and mine detectors.

In more recent times, military dogs have been used to identify improvised explosive devices (IEDs). Lucca, a mixed German shepherd–Belgian Malinois, joined the Marine Corps in 2006. She served two tours of duty in

Jetta, a three-year-old black Labrador, had the job of fetching the morning newspaper and bringing it to Beth and Pat's front door. Jetta was good at his job. However, sometimes the newspaper was not in the driveway. Not wanting to disappoint his owners and fail in his job, Jetta proceeded to collect newspapers from the nearby neighbor driveways. His record was five newspapers in one morning. He especially liked the *Wall Street Journal*, which typically weighed less than the local newspapers and fit easily into his mouth.

Iraq and one in Afghanistan, which included four hundred combat patrols. She is credited with uncovering forty IEDs and saving the lives of many marines. She was severely injured on one patrol, however, and had a leg amputated. She survived and was subsequently retired; she lived with her marine handler and his family until her death.[1]

Search and rescue (S&R) dogs often find survivors in catastrophic conditions, including earthquakes, floods, and so forth. They found many of the 9/11 survivors from the World Trade Center attack in 2001 under the rubble. One S&R dog found Genelle Guzman-McMillan, who was the last survivor found. She had been buried for twenty-seven hours before a dog found her scent and insisted humans dig where she was.

Dogs are also used to solve crimes and catch criminals. Jared Fogel, the former spokesman for Subway, was recently sentenced to more than twelve years in prison for child pornography. What is not commonly known is that the key evidence was found by Bear, a black Lab, who had been trained in sniffing out electronics components and found Fogel's laptop and hard drives filled with incriminating pictures. Bear reportedly was given an extra dog biscuit for the good work.

Dogs are commonly employed as sniffers at airports, identifying people and packages containing illegal drugs or food. When authorities find an

Bam Bam is a big five-year-old German shepherd. Bam Bam looks sinister but is a friendly dog that gets along with everyone on the beach. Bam Bam believes his job is to check everyone's house and make sure everyone is okay. Maybe he learned this from his owner, who is a police officer. As often as possible, Bam Bam gets out and goes from house to house checking for open doors. If someone leaves a door ajar, especially fronting the beach, Bam Bam goes inside and lets the homeowner know he or she forgot to close the door. This is thoughtful, but sometimes people get upset when a big German shepherd shows up in their bedroom unannounced. Whenever we hear a scream emanating from a house on the beach, it is probably just because Bam Bam showed up in someone's bedroom unexpectedly.

illegal substance as a result of an alert dog, the successful dog is given a treat as a reward. This sounds like a great job for a dog. As expected, the sniffer dogs don't miss much.

Dogs contribute to faster healing and better health when they visit hospital patients and retirement home residents. Guide dogs, assistance dogs, and service dogs make life better for blind and disabled people. Dogs have had a significant and favorable effect when introduced to psychiatric hospital patients. Recently, dogs have been introduced in prisons. Inmates who are given the responsibility to care for dogs are more likely to be released early for good behavior and less likely to return to prison after being released.[2]

Milton Gee, a friend and veterinarian, told me that every dog needs a job, whether it's catching a ball or helping someone to find his or her way. Dogs do not take vacations; they work for pats and treats, and they are never in a bad mood. They set the example for everyone.

Work is important for people as well as dogs. Everyone needs something productive to do. Work provides a sense of self-worth—and, generally, a means of income to pay the expenses of life. According to the American Psychological Association, "Our work can be a big part of our identity and offer insights into what is important to us."[3]

---

## Having a job is important to self-esteem and psychological well-being.

---

Often when people meet strangers in a social setting, the first question is, "What do you do?" They are really asking, "What is your job?" Having a job is important to self-esteem and psychological well-being.

According to psychologists, jobs provide the following mental health benefits, among others:

- Feelings of contribution and being appreciated
- The satisfaction of solving problems and learning new things
- Relationships with fellow workers
- Daily routines eliminating mental decisions about what to do next[4]

The preceding list was presented in an article in *Forbes* magazine, which also quoted the May 1998 issue of *Journal of Business Ethics*: "Work is not simply trading labor for dollars. Work is the way we find identity as individuals and how others identify us."[5]

Having a job is not necessarily going to a place of work every day. Stay-at-home parents have a job raising children. Volunteers have jobs, even if they do not provide financial compensation. Marc Chagall, the famous artist, explained, "Work isn't to make money; you work to justify life."[6] The poet Maya Angelou said, "Nothing will work unless you do."[7] Chagall and Angelou did not go to the office every day; they created beauty in paint and words, but they both appreciated the importance of work. Like dogs, everyone needs a job.

When people retire, they leave jobs and careers, but they still need something to do. They need fulfilling activities, whether these include part-time employment, volunteering, sports participation, writing, art, travel, or other avenues. Activities must fill the needs that employment previously provided. Retirement does provide the opportunity to pursue activities that people did not have time to pursue when they were working full time, but they must have the initiative to do this.

Retirement afforded me the time and opportunity to write. I always loved to write, but with work and family demands, there was never time. My friend Kathy Reed always had a talent for painting and studied art in college. But it was not until she retired that Kathy had time to pursue her passion. Similarly, my friend in Australia, Gail McKenzie, is an amazing artist but did not have the time to paint until she cut back her office hours as she approached retirement and made art a priority.

Regardless of the activity selected, it is important to do it well. There is an old, familiar saying that my grandmother often quoted: "A job worth doing is worth doing well." Any undertaking that requires time, effort, and energy should be worth doing to the best of one's ability. Half-hearted efforts are not worthy of one's time and energy.

The value of work has been recognized for centuries. In the Bible, Genesis 2:15 says, "The Lord took the man and put him in the Garden of Eden to work it and keep it," and 2 Corinthians 9:6 says, "Whoever sows sparingly will also reap sparingly, and whoever sows bountifully will also reap bountifully."

The value of work was a topic of Confucius's teaching five hundred years before the birth of Christ. The following observations have been attributed to Confucius and are often quoted: "When you are laboring for others, let it be with the same zeal as if it were for yourself,"[8] and "Choose a job you love, and you will never have to work a day in your life."[9]

Work involves productivity. If work is not productive, why bother? Work includes progress toward measurable results. If results do not lead to something potentially worthwhile, the effort is not worth undertaking.

Work is goal oriented. Often people are too focused on the process and forget the goal is to obtain results. Process is important but only as a path to achieving results.

Work should provide compensation. People are usually compensated financially for their work, but the best goal is not a quest for money; rather, it is a quest for success in what one likes to do. The money follows success. Bill Gates, one of the wealthiest and most successful men in the world, described his early days founding Microsoft with Paul Allen: "Paul and I never thought we would make much money out of the thing. We just loved writing software."[10] Warren Buffet, one of the wealthiest investors in the world, advises, "There comes a time when you ought to start doing what you want. Take a job that you love." He also states, "I think you are out of your mind if you keep taking jobs that you don't like because you think it will look good on your résumé."[11]

Some jobs provide psychological benefits. I serve on a city commission for no salary, but I feel I am giving back to my community. Typically, teachers, nurses, caregivers, and others are paid less than they would be had they joined the corporate world, but they value their contribution and nonmonetary compensation more than higher salaries.

Dogs take on jobs they like to do, and people should replicate this attitude that work should be enjoyable. Work can be its own reward. Steve Jobs, founder of Apple, talked about his love of work: "Your work is going to fill a large part of your life, and the only way to be truly satisfied is to do what you believe is great work. And the only way to do great work is to love what you do."[12] Dale Carnegie, the man who taught millions how to succeed, advised, "People rarely succeed unless they have fun in what they are doing."[13]

Unfortunately, many people work at jobs they do not like because they fear loss of essential compensation if they resign. According to a Gallup poll of working Americans, only about 30 percent are "engaged" in their work, and almost 70 percent are "unengaged."[14] Gallup defines "unengaged" as "checked out," or putting in time without much energy or passion. This leads to lower productivity and poorer results than otherwise achievable, and it is unnecessary and unfortunate for all involved.

If leadership is the ability to inspire others, management shares responsibility for unengaged employees. Better management should lead to increased employee engagement.

In contrast to unengaged workers, dogs are engaged in whatever they do. If they choose to chase a ball, for example, they usually run hard. Otherwise they choose not to chase. A dog would never understand why a human would choose an activity and then not engage. There are so many activities to choose from; people should be able to find something they enjoy doing that is productive.

Dogs and humans should remember that whether they have a job that compensates with money or treats or one that provides other forms of satisfaction, it is important to have fun, engage, and excel. If one cannot do this, one should find another job, even if one is retired.

### Chapter Takeaways

1. Everyone needs a job.
2. Jobs provide monetary and psychological benefits.
3. Any job worth doing is worth doing well.

# 17

# Selecting the Right Leash

© Martin Bucella. Used with permission.

***I do not like leashes;*** *I prefer to run free, like I did in the wild.*

*Most mornings, I walk with Scott to the dog beach in Del Mar where dogs can run off leash with other dogs. I love to run; it is good exercise and allows me to hang out with pack members and meet new dogs. Running and exercising burns off stress, anxiety, and boredom. It makes me tired and sleepy so I don't get into trouble doing other things. Nothing is as good as running free, except maybe finding a special treat.*

*When I am not at the dog beach or a dog park, I usually walk on a leash with Scott. Sometimes we just walk around the neighborhood, and sometimes we take a long walk into town, where he buys a coffee at Starbucks, and I pick up some treats from friendly merchants and their customers.*

*Scott and I went to a few dog trainers, including Hector, until I convinced Scott it was not necessary. Hector is a nice guy, but he recommended a very short leash when walking a dog. He told Scott that dogs like being on a short leash because we live only to serve our master. If you believe this, I have a fire hydrant to sell you.*

*It seems to me the length of the dog's leash should reflect the circumstances. If I am walking near cars, a shorter leash is okay. I am usually too busy sniffing and looking for other dogs to notice cars much. Scott is more likely to notice a car or truck about to run over us.*

*Long leashes can be a problem for walks in areas with frequent trees or signposts. It is too easy to wrap a leash around a bush, tree, or pole, especially if the leash is long. When I am busy sniffing, sometimes I don't notice a tree or other obstacle to avoid.*

*However, in most cases I like a longer leash because it gives me more freedom to explore my surroundings. Longer leashes provide the opportunity for more exercise, although sometimes I get into trouble when I try to chase a cat or another animal when leashed. The other day, I saw a rabbit crossing the street. There was no way Scott was going to hang onto the leash when I bolted toward the bunny. Sometimes leashes are not as constraining as assumed. Unfortunately, I didn't catch the rabbit, but I will be watching for him on future walks.*

*Being on a leash, regardless of size, does not mean a dog will stay out of trouble. Dogs tend to be more aggressive toward other dogs when leashed because we feel more protective of our owners when others approach. Dogs also feel more vulnerable when leashed because we cannot run or escape danger and are therefore more defensive. Sometimes we become tangled in the leashes and feel helpless and threatened.*

*We often misread another dog's intentions when leashed because we cannot fully sniff the other dog. It is not uncommon to see leashed dogs growl and lunge at each other, but that is not normal when dogs are off leash at the park. Rosie is friendly toward virtually all dogs and people when off leash, but she almost always panics and acts aggressive toward others when on a leash. She must have had something bad happen to her on a leash when she was younger.*

\* \* \*

Humans do not wear leashes tethered to another person. But we are constrained by invisible leashes, including laws, regulations, and behavioral norms. We are constrained by societal rules.

People can choose to live on a short leash, where they follow well-traveled paths and rarely deviate. This produces order and conformity. Others choose a longer lead, which allows more exploration, discovery, and creativity. Those who choose a longer leash need to watch for "cars" and other hazards, however, or they could be run over by what they don't see or anticipate.

At times, we can choose to shed the leash completely and seek new places and ideas, charge in new and unexplored directions, define novel solutions, and expand our knowledge and the knowledge of others. These unleashed explorers need to watch out not only for cars but also for known and unknown dangers. What they find may prove beneficial or not; they will not know until they look.

---

## Humans do not wear leashes tethered to another person, but we are constrained by invisible leashes.

---

In personal relationships, one partner sometimes tries to manage or dominate the other partner. He or she wants to keep the partner on a short leash and control the direction and movement. Partners willing to accept dominance appear to fear boredom and seek adventure that they believe will come from being with a dominant partner, according to research presented in *Psychology Today*.[1] Another article in the same publication suggests that partners who try to dominate others cannot control their own behavior.[2] If the submissive partner wants to be on a short leash, that is his or her decision, but he or she should recognize what is happening and make sure that is the life that is desired.

These concepts also apply in business. A controlling or micromanaging boss who keeps employees on a short leash seeks conformity and implementation of specific methods and practices. The boss is primarily concerned with replicating the formula that has presumably worked previously. Fast food workers, for example, follow strict methods and policies that are developed to maximize efficiency and minimize variation in service and food quality between units of the same restaurant chain. The conformity-demanding boss should not expect creativity, change, or improved ways of doing things. Using the tried-and-true path comes at the expense of innovation and progress.

The manager who allows employees a longer leash and more freedom should expect new discoveries, improved methods, more creative solutions,

### Dogs off Leash in New York City

On the *Moth Radio Hour*, Arthur Bradford tells what can happen when you walk your dog off leash where it is illegal to do so. With his dog and a friend, he climbed through a fence in Brooklyn to walk along the waterfront, as many others in the neighborhood did. The police arrived and ordered everyone out of the closed area but checked IDs to see if any had outstanding warrants. Unfortunately, Bradford had received a citation years before from the Parks and Recreation department for having a dog off leash in a city park. He had forgotten all about the citation, but it was on the city's computer. Bradford was arrested, placed in a holding cell, transferred to central booking, and spent the next two nights in jail with many criminals accused of violent crimes while waiting to see a judge. When his fellow inmates asked Bradford what he was accused of, he replied, "Assault." He wanted their respect, and saying, "Dog off leash," did not seem appropriate. The judge finally released him. If you walk a dog off leash in New York City, beware: you could be handcuffed, imprisoned, and treated like a hardened criminal.[3]

and more mistakes. If he or she and the employees learn from the mistakes and avoid cars and other threats, long-term improvements and progress should result.

Some employees may be more self-motivated and better self-managers who need less direction, whereas others may benefit from more direction and more frequent reinforcement. The proper length of the leash should reflect not only the management style and job requirements but also the nature of the affected employees.

Frequently, significant discoveries are made in unexpected places. If scientists were limited to a short-leash environment, they would be unable to broaden their view and find what they would otherwise have likely missed. Alexander Fleming, a Scottish biologist, was working on staphylococci when he took a vacation in 1928. When he returned from holidays, he discovered a fungus had contaminated some of his cultures, and the fungus seemed to kill bacteria. He deviated from his study plan, pursued the new observation, and ultimately discovered penicillin.[4]

Percy Spencer was an American engineer working for Raytheon on a project involving vacuum tubes used to generate microwaves. One day he noticed that a chocolate bar in his pocket melted when he stepped in front of such tubes. His subsequent investigation led to the development of the microwave oven.[5]

John Pemberton, a pharmacist, was trying to develop a cure for headaches. He tried mixing coca leaves and cola nuts. Evidently, his assistant somehow mixed the concoction with carbonated water, which was the start of Coca-Cola.[6] All of these unexpected and unsought discoveries resulted from individuals who were willing to change direction, alter plans, and stray further than would have been possible if leashed to a narrow, inflexible program of inquiry.

People working off leash (and not merely replicating the work of others) have also created many of the recent technological innovations. The new industry leaders in technology like Google and Facebook did not follow prescribed methods and formulas but instead invented new ways of doing things. They were not constrained by conventional leashes.

The newest technological focus in automobiles is automatic driving, where a person does not need to steer the car. When fully developed, the system will permit the passenger to input a destination into the navigation system and be driven there. Most of the early advances in automatic driving are coming from technology firms like Google and Tesla. Traditional automobile manufacturers are beginning to set up research centers in California to work on their own systems, evidently believing the research needs to be done with longer leashes, without being constrained by the established organizational rules and structure.

As managers, keeping employees on short leashes also inhibits teamwork. Dogs work together as a pack and accomplish what no one dog could do alone. People generally work best in teams also, sharing and evaluating different ideas arising from different experiences. Increasingly, business schools require team-based projects as part of their class assignments. This results from the body of research and case studies that have shown teamwork is usually important to accomplish challenging goals, especially in changing conditions and markets. Short leashes and team-based interaction appear to be contradictory and incompatible conditions.

Top-down decision-making can be similar to keeping employees on a short leash. Success in top-down companies depends almost solely on the boss or senior manager, and rarely can one manager make the best decisions consistently when compared to decisions that reflect collective experience and knowledge.

In life, as in business and in the life of dogs, allowing some room to run should result in better outcomes for all, even considering the mistakes that will occur occasionally. It should lead to healthier, happier, and longer lives.

### Chapter Takeaways

1. Keeping a partner on a short leash is a way of exerting dominance.
2. Keeping employees on a short leash results in conformity and consistency.
3. Long leashes or untethered inquiry can result in transformational discoveries.

# 18

# Taking Advantage of opportunities

© Martin Bucella. Used with permission.

**Dogs like me experiment with different activities** and quickly decide what we like to do. Then we do it as much as possible, taking advantage of every opportunity. I like to chase and be chased, but I don't like to retrieve balls or Frisbees. The more I can convince a dog like Chewy to chase, the more fun I have.

When an opportunity arises, like when I find a donut on the beach, I need to be prepared and act quickly. I grab the morsel and run before other dogs that are faster or bigger can steal it. My success depends on taking advantage when opportunities become available.

When Scott puts on his shoes, I run to the front door and plead to go on a walk. I am taking advantage of knowing that Scott is going somewhere. If he lets me go with him, I generally behave so he takes me with him again.

*When Beau and Rosie come over, we run around the driveway and play. Beau or I will pick up a rope and start a tug-of-war. Sometimes Rosie also grabs the rope, and there is a three-way tug. I always take advantage of play times.*

*Sometimes Scott says, "Every dog has his day." I think this applies to dogs and people.*

\* \* \*

In life, people are confronted with big and small opportunities regularly. According to *Merriam-Webster*, *opportunities* represent the favorable junction of circumstances. Taking advantage of opportunities when they occur leads to greater happiness and success in life and in business.

Life coach Adam Sicinski wrote a column on how to make the most of life's opportunities. He recommends six steps to ensure one benefits from future opportunities as they arise:

1. Clarify your goals. Know what you want.
2. Mentally prepare yourself. Acquire the necessary knowledge, skills, support, and tools so you are prepared.
3. Network with people. The more people one knows and interacts with, the more opportunities are likely to emerge.
4. Question everything. Curiosity leads to more opportunities.
5. Recognize the opportunity. Opportunities are frequently made available because they come with associated problems that require hard work and innovative solutions.
6. Take calculated risks. Weigh the pros and cons of actions and then move ahead if the potential positives outweigh the risks.[1]

Often, people do not take advantage of opportunities even when they recognize them. Typical excuses, according to career coach Barbara Seifert, PhD, include the following:

- It's not the right time.
- You don't have the money.
- You might not achieve the desired results (fear of failure).
- You are not deserving of what you desire (lack of confidence).

She recommends being bold and fearless to overcome reluctance and fear of failure or disappointment.[2]

Although opportunities arise periodically, one never knows when he or she will have the opportunity to perform on a bigger stage. When I was working as a senior vice president at the Hahn Company in San Diego during the early 1990s, our corporate owner decided to split the company into two parts: a high-profile namesake company with top-quality fashion shopping malls and a company with lower-quality assets and a history of losing money. I became the CEO of the "bad bank" company, and the better-than-expected performance that followed led to a long, successful career of corporate turnarounds.

When I was CEO of Center America Property Trust in Houston, we had a large loan from Wells Fargo Bank. The loan was secured by a group of shopping centers. I wanted to demolish one center in the loan pool because it was in poor physical condition and required excessive maintenance. I thought a vacant site would be worth more than a dilapidated shopping center, so I called the bank account officer and explained that I wanted to demolish one of the assets securing their loan but was not able to pay down the loan balance. No one at Center America, our board, or the bank account officer thought the bank would approve such an unusual request, but after studying the situation and sending bank staff to look at the site and future plans, Tim Sloan, the senior bank officer responsible for their real estate loans, did agree and approved the demolition. He was a creative, knowledgeable guy who could understand such an unconventional request. The site was later redeveloped and the loan repaid when due. Subsequently, Sloan rose through the ranks of Wells Fargo. When the bank's longtime chairman and CEO, John Stumpf, suddenly and unexpectedly announced his retirement after the bank was discovered to have created false customer accounts, the board turned to Tim Sloan to take the helm. Sloan was prepared and was able to step into a challenging situation.

I knew Craig Perry when I lived in Australia. Craig is an affable guy, has a great sense of humor, works hard, and is intelligent and insightful. He is also a professional golfer, although he does not necessarily look like one. Physically, he is short, overweight, and has large, muscular arms. His nickname on the pro tour was Popeye, probably because of his muscular arms.

In 2004, Craig was playing for the Ford Championship on the PGA tour at the Doral Country Club in Florida. He was tied for the lead with Scott Verplank as the two golfers approached the final hole. Scott hit his shot on the green about thirty feet from the pin. The television commentator, Hall of Fame golfer Johnny Miller, ridiculed Craig, saying, "Perry's swing was enough to make [legendary golfer] Ben Hogan puke." Craig then carefully lined up his approach shot 176 yards from the pin and promptly sunk the shot for an eagle and the Ford championship. It was one of the great shots

Hernando and Susan's dog, Chester, knew how to take advantage of circumstances. He was an active Jack Russell that loved to play soccer. As often as permitted, he played with their girls in the backyard. When he could not push the ball fast enough with his nose, he would pick up the ball, hold it under his chin, and run.

Chester went to every one of the girls' soccer games when they played for a highly competitive La Jolla girls' team. In one important match, Chester became so excited that he managed to slip away from his leash, run onto the field, take the ball, and run down the field. The referee blew the whistle, but Chester was not about to give up the ball. Both teams chased Chester around the field, and finally one player managed to retrieve the ball. Chester was put back on the leash and watched the remainder of the game from the sidelines, but his expert participation on the field did not go unnoticed.

Subsequently, Chester became official team mascot and was a popular figure on Facebook. When he died several years later, tributes poured in from all over the world on Facebook. Chester had used his one opportunity to perform on a greater stage to become famous.

in golf history. When Craig was given an opportunity to perform on the international stage at Doral, he performed brilliantly. Prior to that shot, Craig had prepared through endless hours of practice and lessons: he had turned pro at the age of nineteen and won his first tournament in Australia the same year.

## You never know when you will have the opportunity to perform on a bigger stage.

In the theater and cinema industries, many of the best-known actors started out as understudies to established stage stars. Understudies work hard, memorize parts and lines, and usually receive no recognition. It is a mostly thankless job, but it offers the opportunity to perform onstage if the lead actor is unable to perform. It is critically important to be prepared and take full advantage in the event an opportunity arises.

In 2012 Shirley MacLaine received the American Film Institute's Lifetime Achievement Award, and in 2013 President Obama honored her at the Kennedy Center Honors awards. Previously, she won an Oscar, several Emmys, and numerous other recognitions. She started her career as an understudy to actress Carol Haney in the 1954 production of *The Pajama Game*. When Haney sprained her ankle and could not perform, MacLaine had her opportunity and impressed producer Hal Wallis, among others, leading to a long, successful career.

Anthony Hopkins is considered to be one of the greatest British actors. His awards cover a wide landscape and are too many to mention. He started his long and illustrious career as an understudy to Sir Laurence Olivier. In 1965 when Olivier suffered from appendicitis during a production of *The Dance of Death*, Hopkins had his break, and his career was launched.

In more recent times, a young actress, Sutton Foster, was the understudy in a revival of *Thoroughly Modern Millie* at the nearby La Jolla Playhouse in 2002. When the lead actress became ill, Foster's subsequent performances won her a Tony Award, and she began a successful career onstage and in film.[3]

I never was an actor or even had that aspiration, but I know that when the rare opportunity arises in life and in business, one has to act. I went to Australia in mid-2008 for a one-week visit as a consultant to Morgan Stanley Real Estate Funds. The CEO of Investa Property Group, one of the largest property companies in Australia, resigned the week I was there, and the primary investor asked me to become CEO the same week. I accepted the unexpected assignment; I had no idea the position would be available or offered when I went to Australia, but I was able to perform on the bigger stage because of years of preparation, experience, and visibility with the investors.

There are many stories of athletes who were given a chance to perform when injuries struck others or conditions changed. My favorite baseball player growing up near Chicago was "Mr. Cub," Ernie Banks. Banks went to a high school that did not have a baseball team. He played fast-pitch softball for his church team and was introduced to a scout for the Kansas City Monarchs of the Negro American League. He played for the Monarchs in 1953. After major league baseball was integrated, Banks was given the opportunity to try out for the Chicago Cubs, based on his performance and reputation

 Cooper, the small Goldendoodle, likes to lie on the floor by the front screen door so he can watch anyone walking by. Cooper loves to play and whines whenever a dog or friendly person walks by and he is prevented from joining because of that screen door. The other day, Olive, a black Lab puppy that lives next door to Cooper, escaped his enclosure and headed to Cooper's house, hoping to play. When Cooper did not come out, Olive pushed the screen with his head, separating the screen from the door frame, letting Cooper escape. Cooper never realized one could push the screen open. The two dogs played up and down the street until Cooper's owners, Bob and Jan, noticed Cooper running past their window and brought him back inside.

with the Monarchs. He became the Cubs' first black player and went on to become an all-star for fourteen years. In 1977, he was inducted into the National Baseball Hall of Fame and is one of the most venerated players in the history of baseball.

Sometimes opportunity does not appear despite years of preparation. For every story of actors from modest backgrounds achieving recognition and acclaim, there are many who never experienced such success. The comedian Milton Berle once said, "If opportunity does not knock, build a door."[4] You may have to look for opportunities by moving, changing jobs, acquiring more skills or education, and so on. In 1865, when the east coast of the United States was becoming relatively settled and less land was available for farming, Horace Greeley advised, "Go West, young man."[5] The greater opportunities required relocation—and considerable danger and inconvenience.

Opportunities often arise when problems occur. People who solve problems have greater opportunities than people who manage in the wake of them. A well-repeated (but unverified) quote attributed to Winston Churchill resonates with me: "A pessimist sees the difficulty in every opportunity; an optimist sees the opportunity in every difficulty."[6]

A career is composed of a series of building blocks. A foundation is laid by one's education, early work experiences and knowledge gained, and the professional relationships one has developed. This is true in business, sports, the arts, and virtually every endeavor. It is important to have a good foundation of knowledge and work experience and not to flit from job to job, testing unrelated occupations. Too often, young people starting a career bounce around without developing expertise or professional contacts. This does not build a solid foundation for success.

It is fine to try different career options before choosing an area to focus on and specialize, but for some, the experimentation continues too long and does not lead to a foundation on which to build a career. Such people are less likely to find the opportunity to perform on the big stage because the necessary expertise and knowledge base has not been acquired.

Some people are dreamers; they are always pursuing elusive options without securing anything substantive. I seem to meet a lot of guys at the gym who are always talking about their plans to invent a new, "cannot miss" product or provide a new service that will ultimately make them rich. But they show up at the gym every week, and they don't seem to have become rich in the meantime.

Failure to find and secure the right opportunity often happens to performing artists because in their professions, the availability of job candidates greatly exceeds the supply of jobs. Everyone should pursue his or her dreams, but practicality needs to be acknowledged at some point.

It is okay to dream, but to be successful, one must also be a doer. People who only dream of success rarely experience it. Dreams and wishful thoughts are no substitute for action.

### Chapter Takeaways

1. Most people will have an opportunity to perform on a bigger stage someday.
2. Be prepared for when that opportunity arises.
3. It's okay to dream, but to be successful, one must be a doer.

# 19

# Getting the Basics Right

© Martin Bucella. Used with permission.

**There are a few basic things** that are important, and then there is everything else. Getting the basics right is what I do.

My basic priority is bonding with Scott. I watch out for Scott, and he watches out for and takes care of me. My life revolves around Scott.

When Scott is out, I wait patiently for him to return, watching the front door from my couch. When the garage door goes up, I hear it and run to the door where he comes in. I am there for him. Likewise, when Scott is home and I hear the garage door, I know it must be Patti, and I run to the door to greet her.

At night, I curl up next to Scott or Patti while they watch TV or read. Later, when they go to bed, I run up the stairs and jump onto the bed, waiting for them to join me. I want to be with them always. And they want to be with me.

Another basic priority is doing what I like to do. All the dogs I know are good at something and pursue what they like to do. This focus works to their advantage. My friend Beau, for example, is terrific at catching balls. Beau could run after balls all day without stopping. When Beau is sleeping, sometimes her paws move as she dreams of chasing and catching balls. Beau does not catch Frisbees, however, like some others. Beau knows what she is good at, and that is where she applies her focus and effort.

I like to play, but I am not a big dog, so I cannot play rough with the German shepherds like Mira. However, I am fast, so I can outrun the slower guys who may be bigger and stronger. I can grab a sought-after stick and speed away from Titan, for example, even though he is much bigger and stronger. I like to play keep-away and chase, especially with less agile and slower dogs. It is usually hopeless to play keep-away with Chewy.

The other day I was playing keep-away with my neighbor Shirley's granddaughter, Jordan. Jordan was pretty fast, but I was faster. Once she closed the gap, so I ran off the beach, followed the side road for three blocks, reentered the beach, and sneaked up behind Jordan. Doing what I like to do and what I am good at doing usually includes having a plan.

I also like to have everything organized and in its proper place. For example, I like to drink water from Shirley's big red bowl in front of her house. Her water tastes good. Sometimes she actually uses bottled water to fill the bowl. One time Shirley was away, and the bowl was empty. So, Scott took the bowl to our house, filled it with water, and put it on my driveway. I didn't drink, even though I was thirsty, because the bowl was not in the right place. But when Scott carried the bowl back to Shirley's and put it in its proper place, I drank a lot. The bowl needed to be in the right place, and then everything was fine. Recently, the red bowl has been replaced by a new blue bowl, which I resisted at first, but now I think it is okay as long as it remains in the same place.

Generally, dogs know what we like and what we need. We give our owners and partners unconditional love, and we are loved and cared for by them. We are typically organized and focused, and we always have a plan to get what we want.

\* \* \*

Sadie's "getting the basics right" is an important principle for people and organizations. It represents a key strategic process for defining and accomplishing what one desires in life and at work. The basics include

1. defining priorities or goals,
2. acquiring relevant proficiency and expertise to pursue goals and plans successfully,
3. formulating plans to achieve these goals,
4. focusing efforts to achieve results, and
5. being organized in the pursuit.

Underlying this process is the determination of what one likes to do, what one is good at doing and has a competitive advantage at, and where there is opportunity. This is true for both people and organizations. If one does not enjoy doing something, it should not be a goal or priority to do more. If one does enjoy doing something, but others do it better, the opportunity to achieve success and recognition is limited. And if one likes to do something and is better at doing it than anyone else, there must be an opportunity associated with achievement. If one is the best widget designer in the world, for example, but no one wants widgets, there are better opportunities elsewhere.

Before embarking on a new career, organizational venture, or direction in life, people should ask themselves the following questions:

1. Do you enjoy doing this?
2. Do you have, or can you obtain, the required skills and expertise to be successful?
3. Are you as good as or better than others doing the same activity?
4. Is there sufficient reward if you are successful?

The first step in getting the basics right is establishing goals and priorities. Having goals, priorities, and, subsequently, plans usually requires documenting and periodically reviewing and reevaluating them. Writing down goals and having measurable targets and progress works better than just dreaming about doing things.

As individuals, we have different preferences, likes, and objectives. Our priorities and goals may not be the same, but we all probably share some overriding goals, including taking care of our loved ones, accomplishing something, participating in activities that provide pleasure, and succeeding in what we choose to pursue.

Understanding and prioritizing the needs of one's partner and family is an important priority to achieving a sustainable relationship. Unless there is respect, kindness, understanding, and commitment of time and energy, no amount of business success, money, or accumulated material goods will sustain a personal relationship. Being a good parent should be the utmost priority and is a basic requirement—being a good spouse or partner is not far behind. When one is establishing goals and priorities, family should top the list.

Just as it is for Sadie, loving and being loved is another essential element of life and is implicitly a key priority for humans. We receive love and care as helpless babies and then give love and care to our babies in life's grand cycle. In between, we love and care for our partners, family, and friends. Nothing is more basic or important to the lives we live. Sometimes, in the rush of business and life, we take this priority for granted, which is a mistake.

After setting goals and priorities, developing the expertise to best position oneself to achieve desired results requires practice and perseverance. The importance of mastering basic skills is key in sports like baseball. I coached baseball for several years when my sons were younger. We focused on basic tools like catching the ball, throwing it properly, and basic field positioning. The young players on the team all complained because they thought they knew how to catch and throw and wanted to spend time playing scrimmage games. But we started every practice with the basics and never had a losing season.

It is fascinating to watch golf professionals practice before or after a tournament round. My son Ross and I watched the pros at Torrey Pines, California, practice on the driving range when they were in town for what is now called the Farmers Insurance Open. We saw one of the pros, Justin Rose, hit probably one hundred wedge shots at a nearby flag, stopping to look at how closely each shot landed and then repeating the same stroke. He was honing his skill at short distance shots to the pin.

Getting the basic skills right is the same as blocking and tackling in football. No matter how creatively the plays and plans are diagrammed, if one doesn't block and tackle, the plays are unlikely to work. Repeated practice usually improves needed skills in this regard.

Success in one's career often includes preparation by securing a good education, work experience, and acquisition of essential skills. Skills can include specific work skills—for example, a plumber needs to fix a pipe—or more generic skills such as good writing and communication skills.

Plans to achieve goals and priorities vary depending on the individual and his or her circumstances. For a person suffering from a health setback, for example, the goal may be recovery to a former lifestyle or attaining a life as close as possible to what was previously pleasurable. That goal requires a plan to accomplish this. There are many heartwarming examples of wounded soldiers overcoming devastating injuries to achieve their goals. I spent several months in the San Diego US Naval Hospital in the late 1960s and met many sailors and marines who were injured in Vietnam. Their commitment and focus to regaining their health and resuming their lives was inspiring.

In every instance, the injured veteran set a goal, had a rehab plan, focused on the tasks to rebuild the body and mind, and worked within an organization staffed with experts who had the medical knowledge to assist. The ones who succeeded did not become distracted by feeling sorry for themselves, becoming too dependent on pain medications, or leaving the supportive organizational setting. When someone has a plan and is focused, motivated, and organized, anything is possible.

Similar to individual circumstances, in organizational and business management, a key step is to determine what an organization does well, where there is competitive advantage, and where there is market opportunity. Setting goals and objectives to utilize these factors follows. Next, a plan for implementation must be defined, and all subsequent efforts and attention must be focused on accomplishing the plan, including organizing an experienced team capable of seizing the opportunity. Everything else is a distraction and reduces the possibility of achieving eventual success.

An inclusive process of defining organizational goals and missions often provides a means for colleagues to buy in to the future corporate direction, a clear statement to employees and investors, and a rubric against which to measure future actions. When I arrived at the Investa Property Group in Sydney, the company was organized into several siloed departments with little interaction or cooperation. Our first group exercise was to write a mission statement of who we were and where we planned to take the company. It began the process of employee buy-in, team building, and organization.

Individuals who are not part of an organization should just write down what they do well, what they like to do, and where they have an advantage. They should formulate their wish list, but they should also test that list

Sometimes we could use some more practice before performing in public. Levi is a French bulldog mix. He is a short, stocky young puppy. His mother apparently taught him to squat when he pees, but now he is learning to lift his leg. Unfortunately, he is still mastering the technique. The other morning, he peed on a guy walking past on the beach by mistake. The guy was lost in thought when he felt the warm spray from Levi. Levi's owner apologized, but the guy was not happy. Levi's owner should have had Levi practice peeing with his leg up before coming to the beach.

against their capabilities and willingness to commit time and energy to achieve their goals. The plan to achieve what they want and what they are potentially capable of accomplishing becomes the road map to securing what they want. They do not need to worry about employee buy-in, but they should consider their partners' and family members' needs.

In both personal and organizational situations, distractions inhibit or prevent us from achieving what is a priority or goal. Distractions come in many forms. Sometimes, we are distracted by little, insignificant things that prevent us from achieving significant progress toward our goals. The Greek philosopher Epictetus warned, "In matters of life, many are the things which distract us."[1] Over two thousand years later, in a different vernacular, the businessman T. Boone Pickens said, "When you are hunting elephants, don't get distracted chasing rabbits."[2] Regarding his campaign, former president Barack Obama said, "Trivial things become big distractions."[3] Realizing our goals and what is important to us often requires avoiding or ignoring possible distractions.

When frustrations mount, as they often do when progress is impeded, remember to focus on what is important. No one can do everything that is asked of him or her; it is critical to focus on priorities and steer away from distractions. Otherwise, goals will likely never be realized.

After establishing basic priorities, goals, and plans, implementing the plans helps move lives forward toward realizing what is desired. Taking action in keeping with defined plans is the way to progress on the path to achieving aspirations and life goals. Having goals but no plan to reach those goals is not much different than not having goals at all.

Hope is not a plan. Hoping one will lose weight is not the same as implementing a specific diet plan. Dreaming about getting rich is not the same as working hard and saving money to invest. Hoping to fall in love with a beautiful man or woman is not the same as shaping up, securing a good education and job, and becoming a more attractive prospective partner.

Clarendon Homes, a premier homebuilder in Australia, had an organization designed to deliver nine hundred homes per year in 2008. When the market changed and volumes declined to three hundred homes per year, executives initially did not respond, hoping for return to the good old days of high volumes. Hope may inspire and motivate, but it is not a business plan.

In 2008, when I became CEO of Investa, the company had seven divisions and 680 employees. The company owned office buildings, had multiple investment funds with more than twenty thousand investors, built houses, and did so many things it was hard to keep track of or manage them. It was like Beau, the golden retriever, being asked to catch Frisbees, chase balls, and bark at the postman. Investa's largest division alone was losing $10 million a month. Subsequently, we developed a plan to concentrate Investa's efforts only on its core strengths and became much more focused, with two divisions and 250 employees. Not surprisingly, the streamlined company became highly profitable.

After goals, skills, and plans are set, implementation becomes the priority, and the most important element in implementing plans is focus. For both corporations and individuals, focus is especially important to overcome difficult obstacles. When I worked at Center America in Houston, the company owned one hundred dilapidated neighborhood shopping centers. Local residents probably considered Center America a slum landlord before the company initiated an active rebuilding and redevelopment strategy. The Center America staff meticulously developed a plan for each property, taking into consideration local physical conditions, perceived tenant interest, and neighborhood considerations, including nearby competition and demographics.

If we could not improve a property at Center America, we sold it. We had a laser focus on creating value through redevelopment, and we exited or deemphasized all other activities. This focus and subsequent implementation led to a successful corporate performance and high investment return.

---

## Getting the basics right includes focusing on what one does well and on where there is competitive advantage.

---

In defining plans and implementation strategies, managers who solicit and listen to opinions and recommendations of others generally make better decisions when deciding how to overcome obstacles or confront problems. At an Investa corporate retreat, senior executives watched a video about a family who was stranded in a remote area and confronted by an approaching wildfire. Each executive then wrote down what the family should do to survive.

Next, the executives were put into groups, and each group was asked to agree on a survival strategy for the family. As individuals, over 90 percent of the executives chose actions that resulted in the death of all family members. This was typical, according to the session moderator. However, after debate and discussion, every group defined and recommended a solution that saved the stranded family. Using group dynamics and interaction, managers usually define better solutions.

Obtaining advice from others is also helpful in solving personal problems. Securing professional advice on how to deal with personal challenges allows a person to benefit from another's experience and training. Obtaining advice from friends, colleagues, and experts provides access to more experience and thought than any one individual has. The more eyes and ears that focus on a problem—in personal life and in business—the more likely the best solution will be found.

Focusing on the basics does not mean neglecting future opportunities or standing still. Building on and extending one's expertise into related areas is often the best way to achieve sustainable growth. At Center America, we created a new division charged with developing new shopping centers, leveraging the experience we acquired from our numerous project redevelopments. The new division was successful.

Similarly, it is also possible to redefine the basics in terms of applicable and required skills. I know many people who returned to college after working for some time. They sought to add expertise and access other types of work. My nephew Wade returned to school to obtain his teaching license, and his wife, Jackie, returned to school to become a nurse. They both changed their employment goals and the associated needs and requirements for a successful career.

There are many examples of big companies that strayed from the basics and lost their focus. Both my sons grew up playing with LEGOs. I spent many hours with them building forts, vehicles, and buildings made of the blocks. However, LEGO—this iconic and hugely successful maker of plastic interlocking building blocks for children—almost went bankrupt in 2003 and 2004. The company reported an operating loss of $240 million and was mired in debt.

In the 1990s this previously successful company moved into several new business lines and away from its core business. It developed a clothing line, branded watches, developed video games, developed and promoted a line of action figures and a television show called *Galidor*, created Clikits craft sets for girls, and undertook a variety of other noncore activities.

In 2004, the company owners hired Jorgen Vig Kundstorp to be the new CEO, and a turnaround plan was announced. A key part of the turnaround was to refocus on the company's traditional customer, five- to nine-year-old boys, and return focus and effort to the basic building block business. The company exited all of the noncore, nonessential businesses and streamlined operations. Today, LEGO is again a very successful toy company, focused, profitable, and dominating its market.

Likewise, there are many companies that have remained focused on their basic strengths through many years and have resisted opportunities to move into noncore businesses. When my sons were young boys, I bought furniture at IKEA. The furniture was affordable, had a nice contemporary look, and gave me an opportunity to work together with my sons to assemble their own bedroom furniture. My older son, Andrew, still has his IKEA bed, which is now in his son's bedroom.

IKEA was started by seventeen-year-old Ingvar Kamprad in 1943 in Sweden and is now the world's largest furniture retailer. Kamprad introduced furniture in 1948, and the company has remained focused on selling furniture and ancillary goods for almost seventy years. The first furniture showroom opened in 1953 in Almhut, Sweden; by 2016 there were 373 stores in forty-seven countries. In 1956, an IKEA worker removed the legs of a table so it would fit in the back of a car; from this simple act came the idea of shipping furniture in flat packs for later assembly. The company has been successfully shipping self-assembly furniture packs since the 1950s.

Determine what is most important, and do not forget this. Write it down if necessary. Make sure time and effort are focused on priorities and goals. Too often we forget what is important and we become distracted by what is not that important. Just remember to get the basics right.

## Chapter Takeaways

1. One should set priorities and goals based on what one likes to do, what one is good at doing, and where there is opportunity.
2. Plan and focus efforts.
3. Ignore distractions.

A young Sadie with Ross and Duke.

# 20

# Leaving Your Mark

© Martin Bucella. Used with permission.

*I leave my mark wherever I go for a walk, like when I walk with Scott to the beach in the morning. It might seem like I just mark willy-nilly, but I am careful where and when I mark. Dogs like me use their urine to mark things because we have a great sense of smell. Whenever a dog pees somewhere, even a small amount, all the other dogs can smell it and recognize which of us marked that spot.*

*Dogs mark for lots of good reasons. For instance, male dogs like to let female dogs know that they are around and interested in mating. When a female is in or near heat, she will often leave marks to let the males know she is available and interested. Our pee is free, and the message is direct and simple.*

*Dogs also mark territory, especially males who want everyone to know what a big territory they have and how strong and powerful they are. Often, we pee around the outside or in front of our house to let other dogs know this is our home. When another dog invades our territory and leaves its scent, we mark over the invader's mark to reestablish our primary ownership of the property.*

*When a dog sniffs another dog's pee, and the second dog thinks it is stronger and more powerful, that dog will pee over the first dog's pee. This is the reason someone may see two dogs in the park taking turns peeing on each other's pee. This is what is called overmarking.*

*Some dogs mark just because they are nervous or insecure. If we are unsure how safe our territory is, we will mark more than usual. Dogs that mark inside a house are really insecure. I know a dog that peed all over the place because its owner brought home a cat.*

*Dogs pee when we are on walks, especially familiar paths that we recognize and feel possessive about. Because many dogs can traverse the same paths, dogs do lots of marking. A dog has to be disciplined to hold it in so it can distribute pee in small amounts over long distances.*

*A dog should never mark inside a home. When a dog is acting badly, it is often because it is threatened or insecure.*

*While male dogs and reproductive females do the most marking, I have learned from my male friends how to mark. If males can pee everywhere and leave their message, there is no reason a female dog like me, even if she is fixed, should not have the same opportunity. Sometimes I have balance issues trying to hold up one leg while peeing like the boys, but I manage. Just because I do it a bit differently, it should not be viewed negatively. I achieve the same results, and the dogs in the neighborhood appreciate sniffing my scent.*

\* \* \*

Like dogs, humans leave their marks too. Humans can see pretty well, so we usually mark our territory with fences, walls, and signs like No Trespassing. It would be more efficient to just pee somewhere like Sadie and her friends than to build walls, but I don't think humans are going to change.

We often act similarly to dogs in our desire to demonstrate and communicate success. When one neighbor buys a nice car, the next neighbor may feel obliged to buy a nicer one as well. When one person buys a newer or bigger house, the relatives often look to buy a newer or bigger house too. We call it "keeping up with the Joneses" instead of overmarking, but the intent is the same.

Some dogs can be a bit excessive on the marking. Nanuk used to go to his family's soccer matches and became overly possessive. At one game, he peed on all the low-sitting beach chairs, which made the human spectators angry when they sat down. And when the coach put down his clipboard with the game plans, Nanuk peed on that too. Nanuk got into a lot of trouble, but the other dogs there understood and also tried to pee on the chairs.

Perhaps some humans flash money, drive big, expensive cars, and live in big houses because of insecurity and to compensate for their inability to leave their mark in a simple, less expensive way. Life as a dog is definitely less expensive than as a human.

Human internet dating sites may be similar to a dog marking for mating purposes. Both are a way of messaging others. Unlike an internet dating site, dogs don't have to pay money to find mates or fill out questionnaires. Pee is free, and the message is simple.

People are also protective of their homes, like dogs. In Texas, where I used to live, when someone invaded another's home territory, the guy living there generally had the legal right to shoot the trespasser. Barking at a trespasser and marking one's property seems like a better option than shooting someone.

When humans are insecure, they can act badly, like dogs. They can be aggressive and say angry things. They can attack and criticize others. Like dogs, the solution to bad behavior in humans is often providing greater comfort and security.

Insecure humans can mark inappropriately also. Guys who boast about how good they are, take credit for the work of others, or brag about sexual conquests may be marking to overcome insecurity. They could probably benefit from seeing a professional therapist.

When humans are competing, we also need to learn to be patient and often hold back. Humans have various sayings to describe this, such as saving your ammunition: "Don't expend all your bullets at one time." Similarly, as Sadie said, dogs save some pee for the journey ahead.

Patti's dog Sophie, a miniature pinscher mix, was born and initially raised in a house full of dogs in Mexico with no training or supervision. She had a tough time understanding what behavior was acceptable. After Sophie was rescued, she clearly suffered from insecurity and marked inside her new home. Now she is not allowed upstairs in her house and cannot go on visits to other houses.

## Every person should ask him- or herself, "How and where am I going to leave my mark?"

While dogs' marking of grass or trees is temporary and will be washed away with the next rain, humans have the ability to leave permanent marks. Due to our longer lives and access to greater resources, one person can improve the lives of others—and, in some instances, improve the world for all. Every human should ask what legacy or mark will remain after he or she dies.

Humans can set an example, support their partners, and nurture and teach their children to prepare them for the future. Humans can contribute greatly to the quality of life of their colleagues and employees, contribute to charities serving the needy and less fortunate, and help make education more affordable and accessible. Winston Churchill is often but inaccurately quoted as having said, "We make a living by what we get, but we make a life by what we give."[1] The saying is appropriate and inspirational, regardless of the original author.

Some highly successful people have pledged to donate most of their wealth to charities. Warren Buffett, probably the most successful investor in US history, is believed to have about $50 billion in assets. He has pledged to give away 99 percent of his net worth to charities, including a gift of reportedly $37 billion to the Bill and Melinda Gates Foundation. In 2015, Buffett donated $2.8 billion to five charities.[2] Buffett will leave a big mark after he passes.

Prince Al-Waleed bin Talal, a wealthy Saudi businessman, plans to give away his entire fortune, estimated to be almost $30 billion.[3] Bill Gates, founder of Microsoft, and his wife Melinda are worth almost $90 billion, according to *Fortune*.[4] Their foundation has funded medical research, and as a result there has been significant progress toward eradicating malaria and other diseases.

On a much smaller scale, I have set up a scholarship program to provide funding for eligible university students who qualify for financial aid. Their obligation is to help others in need. This pay-it-forward financial assistance program is described at the website macdonaldscholars.com and has been implemented at the University of North Carolina, Indiana University, University of Michigan, University of San Diego, and Davidson College. I hope to have the program adopted by other universities in time.

Everybody eventually dies, and we cannot take our money with us. Why not use some funds that may not be needed to support a quality lifestyle and provide others with opportunities? Those who benefit will remember the gift, and that memory will live on and potentially affect generations. This is a form of leaving one's mark or legacy.

A person does not need to be wealthy to leave a legacy of improved lives. Olivia Tait graduated from Davidson College in 2009. While in college, she wrote and published a book of children's pictures from around the world, and she used the proceeds from selling the book to fund the development and subsequent operation of a primary school in a village in Ethiopia. Children in this remote village now have a school thanks to the work and determination of this young woman. She left a significant and enduring mark when she was twenty years old. I suspect she will leave many more marks as she continues life's journey.

Leaving a mark does not need to be financial. The teacher who takes extra time to help a student is leaving her or his mark. The policeman who stops to help a stranded motorist and the nurse who pauses from a hectic schedule to comfort and reassure a patient are leaving their marks on people who will remember their kindness and hopefully pass it on. All people can leave a mark, but what will their mark tell others who encounter it? What will be their legacy?

Every person should ask him- or herself, "How and where am I going to leave my mark? What will my mark convey? Will my mark disappear with the first rain, or will it endure?"

### Chapter Takeaways

1. It is important to leave a mark.
2. No one lives forever, and the mark one leaves will define his or her legacy.
3. Everyone should consider whether his or her mark will endure or disappear quickly.

Scott and Sadie in the "minyard" (mini-vineyard). © Coast Highway Photography. Used with permission.

# 21

# Sadie's Twelve Most Important Lessons for a Better Life

© Peter Steusloff. Used with permission

1. A day without play is a bad day.
2. Being part of a pack is better than being alone.
3. You don't need to be the alpha to have a good life.
4. The grass always smells better in the neighbor's yard.
5. Be nice to dogs you pass on your way, because you will pass the same ones on your return.
6. Wagging your tail gets you far more treats than growling or threatening.
7. Be patient and nice with children if you want them to feed you someday.
8. Don't mess in your own house.

9. Watch out for cars.
10. Leave your mark.
11. Love and be loved.
12. Think like a dog.

"Let's go over this again. Anything that hits the floor is yours, with the following exceptions..."

# Notes

## 1. Looking for Treats

1. "Seneca the Younger," Wikiquote, accessed October 13, 2018, https://en.wikiquote.org/wiki/Seneca_the_Younger.
2. Jay Cassano, "The Science of Why You Should Spend Your Money on Experiences, Not Things," *Fast Company*, March 30, 2015, https://www.fastcompany.com/3043858/the-science-of-why-you-should-spend-your-money-on-experiences-not-thing.
3. Mary MacVean, "For Many People, Gathering Possessions Is Just the Stuff of Life," *LA Times*, March 21, 2014, http://articles.latimes.com/2014/mar/21/health/la-he-keeping-stuff-20140322.
4. Cassano, "The Science of Why You Should Spend Your Money on Experiences, Not Things."
5. Stephen Lussier, interview by Michelle Caruso-Cabrera, *Closing Bell*, CNBC, June 2, 2017.

## 2. Being Persistent

1. "Perseverance," Wikiquote, accessed October 13, 2018, https://en.wikiquote.org/wiki/Perseverance.
2. "Henry Ford > Quotes > Quotable Quote," Goodreads, accessed October 13, 2018, https://www.goodreads.com/quotes/904186-if-you-always-do-what-you-ve-always-done-you-ll-always.
3. Oren Harari, *The Leadership Secrets of Colin Powell* (New York: McGraw Hill, 2003), 164.
4. "Mark Twain," Wikiquote, accessed October 19, 2018, https://en.wikiquote.org/wiki/Mark_Twain.

## 3. Communicating Better

1. John Grohol, "9 Steps to Better Communication Today," Psych Central blog, October 6, 2009, https://psychcentral.com/blog/archives/2009/04/14/9-steps-to-better-communication-today/.
2. Meline M. Kevorkian, "Communicating with Children: You Make the Difference," National PTA, accessed September 23, 2017, https://www.pta.org/programs/content.cfm?ItemNumber=1761 (page no longer available).
3. Henry Blodget, "Jack Welch: How to Kick Ass in These Tough Times," *Business Insider*, May 30, 2009, https://www.businessinsider.com/henry-blodget-jack-welch-how-to-kick-ass-when-times-are-tough-2009-5.

4. William Shakespeare, *Hamlet*, ed. Barbara A. Mowat and Paul Werstine, Folger Digital Texts, accessed November 6, 2018, https://www.folgerdigitaltexts.org/html/Ham.html. See act 1, scene 3, line 74.

## 4. Living in the Moment

1. Federation of All Young Buddhist Associations of Japan, *The Teaching of Buddha: The Buddhist Bible; A Compendium of Many Scriptures Translated from the Japanese* (Chiyoda: Kenkyusha Printing, 1934), n.p.

2. Henry David Thoreau, *The Writings of Henry David Thoreau*, vol. 12, edited by Bradford Torrey (Boston: Houghton Mifflin, 1906), 159; via the Walden Woods Project, accessed November 1, 2018, https://www.walden.org/work/the-writings-of-henry-david -thoreau/. Also available at "April 24, 1869," This Date, from Henry David Thoreau's Journal, accessed October 13, 2018, http://hdt.typepad.com/henrys_blog/2010/04/april-24-1859.html.

3. Jay Dixit, "The Art of Now: Six Steps to Living in the Moment," *Psychology Today*, November 1, 2008, https://www.psychologytoday.com/articles/200811/the-art-now-six-steps -living-in-the-moment.

4. "Sati (Buddhism)," Wikipedia, accessed October 13, 2018, https://en.wikipedia.org /wiki/Sati_(Buddhism).

## 5. Planning Your Escape

1. Elka Torpey, "Measuring the Value of Education," *Career Outlook*, Bureau of Labor Statistics, US Department of Labor, April 2018, https://www.bls.gov/careeroutlook/2018/data -on-display/education-pays.htm.

2. DailyMail.com Reporter, "High School Graduates Earn $1 Million Less over a Lifetime Than College Grads (And Picking the Wrong Major Could Cost $3.4m)," May 9, 2015, https:// www.dailymail.co.uk/news/article-3075189/High-school-graduates-earn-1-million-lifetime -graduate-college-new-report-finds.html.

3. "Unemployment Rate 2.5 Percent for College Grads, 7.7 Percent for High School Drop-outs, January 2017," *Economics Daily*, Bureau of Labor Statistics, US Department of Labor, February 7, 2017, https://www.bls.gov/opub/ted/2017/unemployment-rate-2-point-5-percent -for-college-grads-7-point-7-percent-for-high-school-dropouts-january-2017.htm.

4. Juncal Cunado and Fernando Perez de Garcia, "Does Education Affect Happiness? Evidence for Spain," *Social Indicators Research* 108 (2012): 1–12.

5. Fareed Zakaria, *In Defense of a Liberal Education* (New York: W. W. Norton and Company, 2016).

6. Valerie Strauss, "Nelson Mandela on the Power of Education," December 5, 2013, https://www.washingtonpost.com/news/answer-sheet/wp/2013/12/05/nelson-mandelas -famous-quote-on-education/?noredirect=on&utm_term=.8e2c70dbe55.

7. "T. S. Eliot, the Poet, Is Dead in London at 76," *New York Times*, January 5, 1965, https://archive.nytimes.com/www.nytimes.com/books/97/04/20/reviews/eliot-obit.html.

8. Beverly D. Flaxington, "Feeling Stuck in a Relationship," *Psychology Today*, June 16, 2015, https://www.psychologytoday.com/us/blog/understand-other-people/201506/feeling -stuck-in-the-relationship.

9. "The Secret of Getting Ahead Is Getting Started," Quote Investigator, accessed October 13, 2018, https://quoteinvestigator.com/2018/02/03/start/. This saying has been attributed to Mark Twain and also to Agatha Christie as well as earlier anonymous sources.

10. Katie Fehrenbacher, "U.S. Solar Jobs Boom While Oil, Coal Struggle," *Fortune*, January 12, 2016, https://fred.stlouisfed.org/series/CES1021210001.

11. Morgan Watkins, "Even the Kentucky Coal Museum Is Going Solar," *Louisville Courier-Journal*, April 8, 2017, https://www.courier-journal.com/story/news/local/science/environment/2017/04/07/kentucky-coal-museum-shifts-solar-power/100137898/.

12. US Department of State's Bureau of Consular Affairs, *Consular Affairs by the Numbers*, July 2016, https://travel.state.gov/content/dam/travel/CA-By-the-Numbers%202018-Q4.pdf.

## 6. Avoiding Certain Dogs

1. Paul A. Jargowsky and Mohamed El Komi, "Before or After the Bell? School Context and Neighborhood Effects on Student Achievement," Stanford Center for Opportunity Policy in Education, accessed October 13, 2018, https://edpolicy.stanford.edu/sites/default/files/publications/or-after-bell-school-context-and-neighborhood-effects-student-achievement.pdf.

2. Alex Lickerman, "The Importance of Good Influences," *Psychology Today*, April 8, 2010, https://www.psychologytoday.com/us/blog/happiness-in-world/201004/the-importance-good-influences.

3. Princesswithapen, "10 Types of People to Stay Away From: Avoiding Negative Influences and Rude, Depressing People," PairedLife, December 28, 2016, https://pairedlife.com/friendship/10-types-of-people-to-stay-away-from-Avoiding-negative-influences-rude-and-depressing-people.

4. Lawrence J. Peter and Raymond Hull, *The Peter Principle: Why Things Always Go Wrong* (New York: William Morrow and Company, 1969).

5. Anna Voigt, *A Way Forward: Spiritual Guidance for Our Troubled Times* (Philadelphia: Red Wheel, 2003), 110. For more on this quote, see "Three Things Cannot Be Long Hidden: The Sun, the Moon, and the Truth," FakeBuddhaQuotes.com, accessed October 13, 2018, https://fakebuddhaquotes.com/three-things-cannot-be-long-hidden-the-sun-the-moon-and-the-truth/.

6. Takashi Mochizuki, "Toshiba Misstated Operating Profit by $1.2 Billion," MarketWatch, July 20, 2015, https://www.marketwatch.com/story/toshiba-misstated-operating-profit-by-12-billion-2015-07-20.s

## 7. Knowing When to Bark

1. Lisa Juliano, "No One Likes a Complainer. Here's Why," *Psychology Today*, August 2, 2015, https://www.psychologytoday.com/us/blog/contemporary-psychoanalysis-in-action/201508/no-one-likes-complainer-heres-why.

2. Juliano, "No One Likes a Complainer."

3. Kristen Korosec, "Ten Times More Deaths Linked to Faulty Switch Than GM First Reported," *Fortune*, August 24, 2015, http://fortune.com/2015/08/24/feinberg-gm-faulty-ignition-switch/.

4. John Stuart Mill, *On Liberty* (Mineola, NY: Dover, 2002), 9. Originally published 1859.

5. Aesop, *Aesop's Fables* (New York: Fall River Press, 2014).

6. Timothy L. Fort, *Ethics and Governance* (New York: Oxford University Press, 2001).

## 8. Watching Out for Hoses

1. Heraclitus, *The Art and Thought of Heraclitus: An Edition of the Fragments*, ed. Charles H. Kahn (Cambridge: Cambridge University Press, 1981), 105.

2. McKinley Corbley, "Dog Spends Days Protecting Injured Pup from Passing Trains," Good News Network, January 2, 2017, https://www.goodnewsnetwork.org/dog-spends-days -protecting-injuring-pup-passing-trains-watch/.

3. Amie M. Gordon, "5 Tips for Avoiding Conflict in Your Relationship," *Psychology Today*, June 30, 2014, https://www.psychologytoday.com/us/blog/between-you-and-me /201406/5-tips-avoiding-conflict-in-your-relationship.

4. Andrew Blankstein and Monica Alba, "Why Do So Few California Homeowners Have Earthquake Insurance?" NBC News, October 16, 2014, https://www.nbcnews.com/news /investigations/why-do-so-few-california-homeowners-have-earthquake-insurance-n227711.

5. NASA, "Evidence. Facts—Climate Change: How Do We Know?," NASA Global Climate Change, accessed October 13, 2018, https://climate.nasa.gov/evidence/.

## 9. Embracing Change

1. "Heraclitus," Wikiquote, accessed October 14, 2018, https://en.wikiquote.org/wiki /Heraclitus.

2. Terri L. Orbuch, *5 Simple Steps to Take Your Marriage from Good to Great* (Austin, TX: River Grove Books, 2015).

3. Margarita Tartakovsky, "5 Steps to a Successful Marriage," Psych Central, May 17, 2016, https://psychcentral.com/lib/5-steps-to-a-successful-marriage/.

4. Lee Ballentine, "What Is the Percentage of Books Published on Which Publishers Actually Lose Money?," *Forbes*, May 28, 2014, https://www.forbes.com/sites/quora/2014/05/28 /what-is-the-percentage-of-books-published-on-which-publishers-actually-lose-money /#2106aa756d58.

5. Michael Cheang, "Why Are There So Many Movie Sequels?," Star2.com, June 2, 2016, https://www.star2.com/entertainment/movies/movie-news/2016/06/02/why-are-there-so -many-movie-sequels/.

6. "Did Einstein Really Define Insanity As 'Doing the Same Thing Over and Over Again and Expecting Different Results'?," Quora, accessed October 14, 2018, https://www.quora .com/Did-Einstein-really-define-insanity-as-doing-the-same-thing-over-and-over-again -and-expecting-different-results.

7. "Address in the Assembly Hall at the Paulskirche, Frankfurt, 25 June 1963," John F. Kennedy Presidential Library Archives, accessed October 13, 2018, https://www.jfklibrary .org/asset-viewer/archives/JFKPOF/045/JFKPOF-045-023.

8. "Jack Welch on Pursuing Your Passion," Strayer University, accessed October 14, 2018, https://buzz.strayer.edu/career-advancement/jack-welch-pursuing-passion/.

## 10. Being a Good Sniffer

1. "Confucius > Quotes > Quotable Quote," Goodreads, accessed October 14, 2018, https://www.goodreads.com/quotes/2057-you-cannot-open-a-book-without-learning-some thing.

2. Dr. Seuss, *I Can Read with My Eyes Shut!* (New York: Random House, 1978), n.p.

3. Michael Lewis, *Moneyball: The Art of Winning an Unfair Game* (New York: W. W. Norton and Company, 2003).

4. Brian Costa, "Zack Greinke: Baseball's Most Obsessively Prepared Pitcher," *Wall Street Journal*, October 9, 2015, https://www.wsj.com/articles/zack-greinke-baseballs-most -obsessively-prepared-pitcher-1444409548.

## 11. Chasing Cars

1. "Perfect Is the Enemy of Good," Wikipedia, accessed October 26, 2018, https:// en.wikipedia.org/wiki/Perfect_is_the_enemy_of_good.

2. William Shakespeare, *The Taming of the Shrew* (New York: Simon and Schuster, 2004), 4.2.43.

3. Erica Sherman, "Morning Mug," *Blynker*, November 16, 2015, https://bklyner.com /morning-mug-dogs-feel-very-strongly-that-they-should-always-go-with-you-in-the-car -in-case-the-need-should-arise-for-them-to-bark-violently-at-nothing-right-in-your-ear --—-sheepshead-bay.

4. See, for example, Josh Hafner, "Does Money Equal Happiness? It Does, but Only until You Earn This Much," *USA Today*, February 26, 2018, https://www.usatoday.com/story/money /nation-now/2018/02/26/does-money-equal-happiness-does-until-you-earn-much/374119002/.

5. Grenville Kleiser, *Dictionary of Proverbs* (New Delhi: APH, 2005), 266.

6. Robert W. Fuller, "Why Do We Want to Be Famous?" *Psychology Today*, September 25, 2009, https://www.psychologytoday.com/us/blog/somebodies-and-nobodies/200909/why -do-we-want-be-famous.

## 12. Earning Trust and Choosing Partners

1. Casey Stengel, "Casey Stengel: Greatest Character of the Game," Casey Stengel Baseball Center, accessed September 23, 2017, https://caseystengel.org/casey.

2. "Martin Luther King Jr. Quotes: In His Own Words," *Birmingham Times*, January 15, 2018, https://www.birminghamtimes.com/2018/01/some-of-dr-martin-luther-king-jr-s-pro found-quotes/.

3. Megan Tschannen-Moran, *Trust Matters: Leadership for Successful Schools* (San Francisco: Jossey-Bass, 2014).

4. Teresa S. Collet, "Being Older Doesn't Make Divorce Any Wiser: Families like Mine Fight to Buck Divorce Trend," September 6, 2018, https://www.usatoday.com/story/opinion /voices/2018/09/06/gray-divorce-elderly-couples-marriage-column/1183820002/.

5. "Kenny Anderson (Basketball)," Wikipedia, accessed October 14, 2018, https:// en.wikipedia.org/wiki/Kenny_Anderson_(basketball).

## 13. Eat, Sleep, Play

1. National Institute of Diabetes and Digestive and Kidney Diseases, "Overweight & Obesity Statistics," October 2012, https://www.niddk.nih.gov/health-information/health-statistics/overweight-obesity.

2. American Diabetes Association, "The Cost of Diabetes," March 6, 2013, www.diabetes.org/advocacy/news-events/cost-of-diabetes.html.

3. Centers for Disease Control and Prevention, "Stroke Statistics," May 9, 2017, https://doi.org/10.1161/01.ATV.0000089628.63625.D4.

4. "Dog Food Diet," People of Walmart, accessed September 23, 2017, http://www.peopleofwalmart.com/dog-food-diet/.

5. *National Vital Statistics Reports* 66, no. 6, November 27, 2017. Published by the US Department of Health and Human Services, Centers for Disease Control and Prevention, National Center for Health Statistics, National Vital Statistics System.

6. "Sleep Deprivation and Deficiency," National Heart, Lung, and Blood Institute, National Institute of Health, US Department of Health and Human Services, accessed October 15, 2018, https://www.nhlbi.nih.gov/health-topics/sleep-deprivation-and-deficiency.

7. Sanjay Gupta, "5 Things You Can Do About a Bad Night's Sleep," *Everyday Health*, accessed October 15, 2018, https://www.everydayhealth.com/news/things-you-can-do-about-bad-sleep/.

8. Camille Peri, "10 Things to Hate about Sleep Loss," WebMD, accessed October 15, 2018, https://www.webmd.com/sleep-disorders/features/10-results-sleep-loss#1.

9. "Sleep," Memory and Aging Center, Weill Institute for Neurosciences, accessed October 15, 2018, https://memory.ucsf.edu/sleep.

10. Mayo Clinic Staff, "Napping: Dos and Don'ts for Healthy Adults," Mayo Clinic, accessed October 15, 2018, https://www.mayoclinic.org/healthy-lifestyle/adult-health/in-depth/napping/art-20048319.

11. "Napping," National Sleep Foundation, accessed October 18, 2018, https://www.sleepfoundation.org/sleep-topics/napping.

12. "Understanding the Side Effects of Sleeping Pills," WedMD, accessed October 18, 2018, https://www.webmd.com/sleep-disorders/guide/understanding-the-side-effects-of-sleeping-pills#1.

## 14. Being Loyal

1. Linda and Charley Bloom, *Happily Ever After . . . and 39 Other Myths about Love* (Novato, CA: New World Library, 2016).

2. Linda and Charlie Bloom, "Got Loyalty?" *Psychology Today*, June 10, 2016, https://www.psychologytoday.com/us/blog/stronger-the-broken-places/201606/got-loyalty.

3. Alexander Pope, letter to Henry Cromwell, October 19, 1709, in *The Correspondence of Alexander Pope*, vol. 1, ed. George Sherburn (Oxford: Oxford Scholarly Editions, 1956).

4. Christopher Hitchens, *The Portable Atheist: Essential Readings for the Nonbeliever* (Boston: Da Capo Press, 2007), 4.

5. Joshua L. Mark, "Dogs in the Ancient World," *Ancient History Encyclopedia*, June 21, 2014, https://www.ancient.eu/article/184/dogs-in-the-ancient-world/.

## 15. Training People

1. Cesar Millan and Melissa Jo Peltier, *Cesar's Rules: Your Way to Train a Well-Behaved Dog* (New York: Three Rivers, 2010), 1.
2. Nathan Bailey, *Divers Proverb 1721* (Halethorpe: Free State Books, 2011), n.p.
3. Plato, *The Laws*, bk. 1, trans. Benjamin Jowett, Internet Classics Archive, MIT, accessed November 5, 2018, http://classics.mit.edu/Plato/laws.1.i.html.
4. Nicholas Kristof, "The Value of Teachers," *New York Times*, January 11, 2012, https://www.nytimes.com/2012/01/12/opinion/kristof-the-value-of-teachers.html.
5. "Howard Schultz, CEO, Starbucks," CNN, December 28, 2007, http://edition.cnn.com/2007/BUSINESS/12/21/boardroom.schultz/.

## 16. Everyone Needs a Job

1. "Lucca (dog)," Wikipedia, accessed September 23, 2017, https://en.wikipedia.org/wiki/Lucca_(dog).
2. Christopher Zoukis, "PAWS Cell Dog Training Program," PrisonEducation.com, April 21, 2012, https://prisoneducation.com/prison-education-news/paws-cell-dog-training-program-html/.
3. Kirsten Weir, "More Than Job Satisfaction," *American Psychological Association Monitor* 44, no. 13 (2013): 39.
4. Mike Lewis, "Life after Retirement—What Do I Do Now?" *Forbes*, October 22, 2013, https://www.forbes.com/sites/mikelewis/2013/10/22/life-after-retirement/#4482ea381677.
5. Lewis, "Life after Retirement"; see also Al Gini, "Work, Identity, and Self: How We Are Formed by the Work We Do," *Journal of Business Ethics* 17, no. 7 (May 1998): 707–14.
6. "Marc Chagall, born Moishe Shagal," Great Thoughts Treasury, accessed October 15, 2018, http://www.greatthoughtstreasury.com/author/marc-chagall-born-moishe-shagal?page=2.
7. Colleen Curry, "Maya Angelou's Wisdom Distilled in 10 of Her Best Quotes," ABC News, May 28, 2014, https://abcnews.go.com/Entertainment/maya-angelous-wisdom-distilled-10-best-quotes/story?id=23895284.
8. Asad Meah, "35 Inspirational Confucius Quotes on Success," Awaken the Greatness Within, accessed October 15, 2018, https://awakenthegreatnesswithin.com/35-inspirational-confucius-quotes-on-success/.
9. "Confucius," Wikiquote, accessed October 15, 2018, https://en.wikiquote.org/wiki/Confucius.
10. Richard St. John, *Stupid, Unlucky and Rich: Spike's Guide to Success* (Toronto: Train of Thought Arts, 2005), 39.
11. Brian Flores, "Warren Buffet: Take a Job That You Love," NASDAQ, April 22, 2016, https://www.nasdaq.com/article/warren-buffett-take-a-job-that-you-love-cm610294.
12. Steve Jobs, Stanford commencement address, June 12, 2005; transcript via "'You've Got to Find What You Love,' Jobs Says," Stanford News, June 14, 2005, https://news.stanford.edu/2005/06/14/jobs-061505/.
13. Dale Carnegie, *The Best of Dale Carnegie Vol-1* (New Delhi, India: Prabhat Prakashan, 2017).

14. Amy Adkins, "Employment Engagement in U.S. Stagnant in 2015," Gallup, January 13, 2016, http://www.gallup.com/poll/188144/employee-engagement-stagnant-2015.aspx.

## 17. Selecting the Right Leash

1. Gwendolyn Seidman, "Why Some of Us Seek Dominant Partners," *Psychology Today*, May 8, 2015, https://www.psychologytoday.com/us/blog/close-encounters/201505/why-some -us-seek-dominant-partners.

2. David Schnarch, "People Who Can't Control Themselves Control the People around Them," *Psychology Today*, May 23, 2011, https://www.psychologytoday.com/us/blog/intimacy -and-desire/201105/people-who-cant-control-themselves-try-control-others.

3. Arthur Bradford, "Dog Off Leash," in *The Moth*, podcast, August 11, 2015, 6:51, https:// themoth.org/podcast/august-11-2015.

4. "Alexander Fleming," Wikipedia, accessed October 15, 2018, https://en.wikipedia.org /wiki/Alexander_Fleming.

5. "Percy Spencer," Wikipedia, accessed October 15, 2018, https://en.wikipedia.org/wiki /Percy_Spencer.

6. "John Pemberton," Famous Inventors, accessed October 15, 2018, https://www.famous inventors.org/john-pemberton.

## 18. Taking Advantage of Opportunities

1. Adam Sicinski, "How to Make the Most of Life's Opportunities," IQ Doodle, accessed September 23, 2017, https://iqdoodle.com/life-opportunities/.

2. Barbara Seifert, *Taking Advantage of Opportunities in Front of You*, The Work at Home Woman, accessed September 23, 2017, http://www.theworkathomewoman.com/taking -advantage-of-opportunities/.

3. Logan Culwell-Block, "Shirley MacLaine, Elaine Stritch and More! The Stars You Never Knew Started Out as Understudies," Playbill, June 21, 2015, http://www.playbill.com /article/shirley-maclaine-elaine-stritch-and-more-the-stars-you-never-knew-started-out -as-understudies-com-351173; "Understudy," Wikipedia, accessed October 15, 2018, https:// en.wikipedia.org/wiki/Understudy.

4. Michael Essany, *The Devil Can't Cook Spaghetti: Using Faith to Overcome Fear* (Hidden Spring, 2009), loc. 612 of 1291, Kindle.

5. "Go West, Young Man," Encyclopedia.com, accessed October 15, 2018, https://www .encyclopedia.com/history/dictionaries-thesauruses-pictures-and-press-releases/go-west -young-man-go-west.

6. Richard M. Langworth, "Churchill on the Pessimist and the Optimist," Richard Langworth.com, June 20, 2017, https://richardlangworth.com/optimist-pessimists.

## 19. Getting the Basics Right

1. Epictetus, *The Discourses of Epictetus with the Encheiridion and Fragments* (London: Forgotten Books, 2012), 77.

2. T. Boone Pickens (@boonepickens), "When you are hunting elephants, don't get distracted chasing rabbits," Twitter, March 7, 2011, 8:15 a.m., https://twitter.com/boonepickens/status/44763192924192768?lang=en.

3. Barack Obama, Speech to the Democratic National Convention, Philadelphia, Pennsylvania, September 6, 2012; see "Transcript: President Obama's Convention Speech," NPR, September 6, 2012, https://www.npr.org/2012/09/06/160713941/transcript-president-obamas-convention-speech.

## 20. Leaving Your Mark

1. "Quotes Falsely Attributed to Winston Churchill," International Churchill Society, accessed October 15, 2018, https://winstonchurchill.org/resources/quotes/quotes-falsely-attributed/.

2. Jonathan Chew, "Warren Buffet Donates $2.8 Billion . . . Again," *Fortune*, July 6, 2015, http://fortune.com/2015/07/06/warren-buffett-donation/.

3. Jonathan Chew, "Saudi Prince Alwaleed bin Talal Is Donating His Entire $32 Billion Fortune," *Fortune*, July 1, 2015, http://fortune.com/2015/07/01/saudi-prince-alwaleed-donation/.

4. Don Reisinger, "Bill Gates' Net Worth Has Hit a Record High," *Fortune*, August 22, 2016, http://fortune.com/2016/08/22/bill-gates-net-worth/.

# Scott's Acknowledgments

To my sons, Andrew and Ross, of whom I am so proud to be their father; my wonderful daughter-in-law, Davida; and my almost-perfect grandchildren, Claire and James. I am truly fortunate.

To Patti Kurtz, who taught me what it means to have someone close who is kind, supportive, and loving.

To Gary Dunham and his colleagues at Indiana University Press for courage and confidence in taking on this unconventional project.

To Indiana University and the University of North Carolina for providing me with a first-rate education.

To Marty Bucella, cartoonist extraordinaire, for the drawings in this book; David Davis, who designed the book cover and layout of the chapters; and Peter Steusloff, the photographer who took many of the photographs of Sadie.

Thank you.

# Sadie's Acknowledgments

To my neighbors:

Shirley Wollerman, who always has treats and a bowl of fresh water for me

Joni and Van Mankwitz, who always have great dog treats whenever I stop by

To my dog sitter and friend, Deeba Van Overberghe

To my dog friends on the beach and in my neighborhood and their (owners):

Beau (Beth and Pat Steusloff)

Rosie (Rick and Marcia Gold)

BJ (David Cohen)

Bailey (Teri and Jim Coker)

Barley (Lynn and Charlie Gaylord)

Bhavi, Bodie, and Max (Vicki Welch)

Brownie (Bart Bowen)

Bru (Betsy Winsett)

Cannoli (Ross and Angie Neglia)

Caesar (Cynthia Bolker and Greg Rizzi)

Chewy (Janet Holcomb)

Coach (Monica and Dean Meredith)

Cooper (Bob and Jan Fillion)

Finn (Hanna Hanna)

Gabby (Tom and Debbie Tucker)

JJ and Willie K (Marla and Bill Engel)

Lucy and Callie (Dan and Robin Crabtree)

Marshall (Ruth and Ed Evans)

Mira (Klaus and Dagmar Gubernator)

Nola (Aaron Brand)

Otis (Tanya Xavier)

Parducci (Ted and Ann Gay)

Riley (Marty and Jim Gigler)

Rigby (Jim Diethrich)
Tag and Devon (Bill and Sharon Scheele)
Titan (Kathy Reed)

To other friends who take me for walks when Scott is not home, including:
Michael McGary

SCOTT MACDONALD has had a successful career working on commercial real estate projects throughout the world. He has been CEO of several companies, including, most recently, Investa Property Group in Sydney, Australia. Before that, he was President of New Plan Excel in New York City; CEO of Center America Property Trust in Houston, Texas; and CEO of affiliated companies of Trizec Hahn in San Diego, California. He was a longtime advisor to Morgan Stanley Real Estate Funds in London and New York. Scott is author of *Saving Investa: How an Ex-Factory Worker Helped Save One of Australia's Iconic Companies*.

SADIE was born near Beaumont, Texas; she never knew her father (and her mother might not have known him either). She and her mom were homeless for the first six months of Sadie's life. Then she was picked up by Beaumont Animal Control (the police), taken to the animal shelter (jail), photographed, and had her (mug) shot put on the internet. When no one claimed her, she was given to a local dog rescue service (foster parents) and eventually adopted by Ross, a law student at the University of Texas in Austin. When Ross accepted a new job in Houston, Sadie was sent to California to live with Ross's father, Scott, where she adapted to and took charge of Scott's home and life.